The Tale of Hreidarr the Fool

Original Text, Translations, and Word Lists

Translated by
Matthew Leigh Embleton

Copyright ©2025 Matthew Leigh Embleton. All rights reserved.

The Tale of Hreidarr the Fool

The Tale of Hreiðarr the Fool *(Old Norse)*..4
Word List *(Old Norse to English)*..35
Word List *(English to Old Norse)* 49
The Tale of Hreiðarr the Fool *(Old Icelandic)* 60
Word List *(Old Icelandic to English)*...90
Word List *(English to Old Icelandic)*...104
A Word Comparison of Old Norse and Old Icelandic Words 115

Cover: Old Norse text over an outline of Iceland. Author's design.

The original Old Norse and Old Icelandic texts are in the public domain.
These translations ©2022 Matthew Leigh Embleton
©2025 Matthew Leigh Embleton (This Edition)

Acknowledgments

I have long been fascinated by languages and history, and I am very grateful to the special people in my life who have supported and encouraged me in my work. Thank you for believing in me. You know who you are.

Introduction

Old Norse is a North Germanic language spoken by inhabitants of Scandinavia from about the 7th to the 15th centuries. Old Icelandic is a variety of Old West Norse that emerged during the Norse settlement of Iceland in the second half of the 9th century. The rich tradition of Icelandic literature survived by oral tradition over several centuries before being written down in the 13th Century. The Tale of Hreiðarr the Fool (*Hreiðars þáttr heimska*) is one of the many Tales of Icelanders or *Íslendingaþættir*. The word '*þáttr*' (plural: '*þættir*') translates as a strand of rope or a yarn, comparable to the word 'yarn' in English sometimes used to refer to a story.

This book contains:
- The Tale of Hreiðarr the Fool (*Hreiðars þáttr heimska*) (Old Norse Version)
- An Old Norse to English Word List
- An English to Old Norse Word List
- The Tale of Hreiðarr the Fool (*Hreiðars þáttr heimska*) (Old Icelandic Version)
- An Old Icelandic to English Word List
- An English to Old Icelandic Word List
- A Word Comparison of Old Norse and Old Icelandic words

The texts are presented in their original form, with a literal word-for-word line-by-line translation, and a Modern English translation, all side-by-side. In this way, it is possible to see and feel how the worked and how it has evolved. This book is designed to be of use and interest to anyone with a passion for the Old Norse or Old Icelandic language, Norse history, or languages and history in general.

The Tale of Hreiðarr the Fool (*Old Norse*)

Old Norse	Literal	English
1	**1**	**1**
Þórðr hét maðr.	Thord was-named a-man.	There was a man named Thord.
Hann var Þorgrímsson, Hreiðarssonar, þess er Glúmr vá.	He was Son-of-Thorgrim, Son-of-Hreidar, this whom Glum killed.	He was the son of Thorgrim, the son of Hreidar who killed Glum.
Þórðr var lítill maðr vexti ok vænn.	Thord was a-little man grown and handsome.	He was a small man in size and handsome.
Hann átti sér bróður, er Hreiðarr hét.	He had himself a-brother, who Hreidar was-named.	He had a brother, who was named Hreidar.
Hann var ljótr maðr ok varla sjálfbjargi fyrir vits sökum.	He was ugly man and scarcely self-supported for wits sake.	He was an ugly man and he could scarcely take care of himself.
Hann var manna frávastr ok vel at afli búinn ok hógværr í skapi, ok var hann heima jafnan.	He was a-man swift and well to strength prepared and humble in character, and was he at-home always.	He was a fast man and very strong, and humble in character, and he was always at home.
En Þórðr var í förum ok var hirðmaðr Magnúss konungs ok mazt vel.	But Thord was in travelling and was court-man Magnus the-king and most well.	But Thord was a travelling man, and a court man of King Magnus who thought most well of him.
Ok eitt sinn, er Þórðr bjó skip sitt í Eyjafirði, þá kom Hreiðarr þar, bróðir hans.	And once his, was Thord prepared ship his in Eyjafjord, then came Hreidar there, brother his.	And one day when Thord was preparing his ship in Eyjafjord, then came Hreidar his brother.
Ok er Þórðr sá hann, spurði hann, hví hann væri þar kominn.	And when Thord saw him, asked he, why he was there coming.	And when Thord saw him, he asked why he had come there.
Hreiðarr segir:	Hreidar said:	Hreidar said:
"Eigi nema erendit væri".	"Nothing except errand was".	"I would not have come unless I had business".
"Hvat villtu þá?"	"What will-you then?"	"What do you want then?"
segir Þórðr.	said Thord.	said Thord.

The Tale of Hreiðarr the Fool (Old Norse)

Old Norse	Literal	English
"Ek Vil fara útan",	"I Wish travel out",	"I wish to travel abroad",
segir Hreiðarr.	said Hreidar.	said Hreidar.
Þórðr mælti:	Thord spoke:	Thord spoke:
"Ekki þykkir mér þér fallin förin".	"Not think I you fallen for-travelling".	"I don't think you are destined for travelling".
Vil ek heldr þat til leggja við þik, at þú hafir föðurarf okkarn, ok er þat hálfu meira fé en þat, er ek hefi í förum".	Wish I rather that to let from you, that you have inheritance ours, and is that half more money than that, which I have in trading-voyages".	"I wish rather than to let you go, for you to have our inheritance, and that is more than half the money which I have in trading voyages".
Hreiðarr svarar:	Hreidar answered:	Hreidar answered:
"Þá er lítit vit mitt",	"Then would little know me",	"Then I would know little",
segir hann, "ef ek tek þenna fjárskakka til þess at gefa mik svá upp sjálfan ok láta þína umsjá, ok mun þá hverr maðr draga af mér fé okkart, alls ek kann engi forræði, þau er nýt eru.	said he, "if I took that uneven-share to this to gave I so up myself and left your guidance, and would then every man draw of me money ours, all I know no self-control, then where used they-are.	he said, "if I took that uneven share, then gave myself up and left your guidance, and then every man would cheat money out of us, and I know no self-control where they are used.
Ok era þér þá betra hlut í at eiga, ef ek ber á mönnum eða gerik aðra óvísu þeim, er um fé mitt sitja at lokka af mér, en eftir þat sé ek barðr eða meiddr fyrir mínar tilgerðir, enda er þat sannast í, at þér mun torsótt at halda mér eftir, er ek vil fara".	And are you then better share in that own, if I bear to people or do other unknown them, is about money mine sit that lure off me, but after that so is beat or hurt for mine to-do, and is that true in, that you should difficulty that rather to-me after, that I will travel".	And it is better for you to own a share, if I bear to people or do otherwise unknown things to them, those who attend in luring money away from me, but after that I will be beaten or hurt for my deeds, for that is true, that you will have a hard time keeping me, when I want to go".
"Vera kann þat",	"Be can that",	"That may be",
segir Þórðr, "en get ekki þá um ferð þína fyrir öðrum mönnum".	said Thord, "but mention not then about travel yours before other people".	said Thord, "but don't mention your travel in front of other people".
Því hét hann.	Therefore promised he.	Therefore he promised.

The Tale of Hreiðarr the Fool (Old Norse)

Old Norse	Literal	English
Ok þegar er þeir eru skilðir, þá segir Hreiðarr hverjum, er heyra vill, at hann ætlar útan at fara með bróður sínum.	And as-soon-as that they were parted, then told Hreidar everyone, that heard would, that he intended out to travel with brother his.	And as soon as they had parted, Hreidar told everyone that would hear him, that he intended to travel abroad with his brother.
Ok firna allir Þórð um, ef hann flytr útan afglapa.	And criticised all Thord about, if he transport out fool.	And everyone criticised Thord, if he travel abroad with such a fool.

2

Old Norse	Literal	English
Ok er þeir eru búnir, sigla þeir í haf ok Verða vel reiðfara, koma við Björgyn, ok þegar spyrr Þórðr eftir konungi, ok var honum sagt, at Magnús konungr var í bænum ok hafði skömmu áðr komit ok vildi eigi láta kæja sik samdægris, þóttist þurfa hvíldar, er hann var nýkominn.	And when they were prepared, sailed they to sea and Became well voyage, came to Bergen, and there asked Thord after the-king, and was he told, that Magnus the-king was in residence and had recently returned come and willed not be-allowed disturbed him same-day, thought needed rest, when he was newly-come.	And when they were ready, they sailed to sea and began their voyage well, they came to Bergen, and there Thord asked for the king, and he was told that King Magnus was in residence and had recently returned home and did not wish to be disturbed that day, because he needed rest after newly coming home.
Brátt litu menn Hreiðar, at hann var afbragð annarra manna.	Soon noticed people Hreidar, that he was stood-out other men.	Soon people noticed Hreidar, that he stood out from other men.
Hann var mikill ok ljótr, ómállatr við þá, er hann hitti.	He was tall and ugly, chatty with then, who he met.	He was tall and ugly, and chatty with whoever he met.
Ok snemma um morgininn, áðr menn Væri vaknaðir, stendr Hreiðarr upp ok kallar:	And early about morning, before people Were woken, stood Hreidar up and called:	And early in the morning, before people were awake, Hreidar stood up and called:
"Vaki þú, bróðir.	"Wake you, brother.	"Wake up, brother.
Fátt veit sá, er sefr.	Little knows so, who sleeps.	He who sleeps knows little.
Ek veit tíðendi, ok heyrðak áðan læti kynlig".	I know news, and heard earlier noise strange".	I have some news, and earlier I heard a strange noise.
"Hverju var líkast?"	"What was like?"	"What was it like?"
spyrr Þórðr.	asked Thord.	asked Thord.
"Sem yfir kykvendum",	"Like about some-beast",	"Like some beast",

The Tale of Hreiðarr the Fool (Old Norse)

Old Norse	Literal	English
segir Hreiðarr, "ok þaut við mjök, en aldri veit ek, hvat látum var".	said Hreidar, "and shrill as much, but never knew I, what have was".	said Hreidar, "and as shrill as one, but I never knew what it was".
"Lát eigi svá undarliga",	"Have not so strange",	"That is not so strange",
segir Þórðr.	said Thord.	said Thord.
"Þat mun verit hafa hornblástr".	"It must been have trumpet-blast".	"It must have been a blast from a trumpet".
"Hvat skal þat tákna?"	"What shall it betoken?"	"What does that mean?"
spyrr Hreiðarr.	asked Hreidar.	asked Hreidar.
Þórðr svarar:	Thord answered:	Thord answered:
"Blásit er jafnan til móts eða til skipdráttar".	"Trumpet-blast is always to meetings or to ship-launching".	"A trumpet blast always means a meeting being summoned or for the launching of ships".
"Hvat táknar mótit?"	"What taken meetings?"	"What are these meetings taken for?"
spyrr Hreiðarr.	asked Hreidar.	asked Hreidar.
"Þar eru dæmð vandamál jafnan",	"They are to-deem disputes equally",	"They are to judge disputes equally",
segir Þórðr, "ok slíkt talat, sem konungr þykkist þurfa, at fyrir alþýðu sé upp borit".	said Thord, "and such told, as the-king seems needed, that before the-people so up bear".	said Thord, "and for things to be told, such as the king sees fit, to bear to the people".
"Hvárt mun konungr nú á mótinu?"	"Whether shall the-king now at meeting?"	"Will the king be there now at the meeting?"
spyrr Hreiðarr.	asked Hreidar.	asked Hreidar.
"Þat ætla ek víst",	"That suppose I certainly",	"I suppose so, certainly",
svarar Þórðr.	answered Thord.	answered Thord.
"Þangat verð ek þá at fara",	"From-here worth I then to go",	"Then it is worth me going there",

The Tale of Hreiðarr the Fool (Old Norse)

Old Norse	Literal	English
segir Hreiðarr, "því at ek vilda þar koma fyrst, er ek sæja sem flesta menn í senn".	said Hreidar, "because that I wish there to-come first, that I see as most people to together".	said Hreidar, "because I wish to go there first, to see as many people together at once".
"Þá skýtr í tvau horn með okkr",	"Then throws to two corners with us",	"Then that throws into two corners with us",
segir Þórðr.	said Thord.	said Thord.
"Mér þætti því betr er þú kæmir þar síðr, er fjölmennt væri, ok vil ek hvergi fara".	"To-me seems therefore better that you come there less, when crowded will-be, and wish I nowhere to-go".	"It seems better to me therefore that you go there less, when it will be crowded, and I don't wish to go there myself".
"Ekki tjáir slíkt at mæla",	"Not express such to discuss",	"It does not do to say such a thing",
segir Hreiðarr, "fara skulum vit báðir.	said Hreidar, "travel shall we both.	said Hreidar, "we shall travel both.
Muna þér betra þykkja, at ek fara einn, en ekki fær þú mik lattan þessarar farar".	Should you better to-think, that I travel alone, and not can you me dissuade this-kind-of journey".	I think you had better realise, that I am going alone, and you can not dissuade me from making this journey".
Hleypr Hreiðarr á brott.	Ran Hreidar to away.	Then Hreidar ran away,
En Þórðr sér nú, at fara mun verða, ok ferr hann eftir, er Hreiðarr ferr hart undan, ok er mjök langt milli þeira.	When Thord saw now, that going should be, also went he after, as Hreidar went hard away, and was much long between them.	But now Thord saw that this would happen, he also went after him, as Hreidar went hard away, and there was a long way between them.
Ok er Hreiðarr sér, at Þórðr fór seint, þá mælti hann:	And when Hreidar saw, that Thord went slowly, then spoke he:	And when Hreidar saw, that Thord was going slowly, then he spoke:
"Þat er þó satt, at illt er lítill at vera, þá er aflit nær ekki.	"It is though true, that bad is small to be, then that strength near is-not.	"It is true that it is bad to be small, because then strength is not near.
En þó mætti vera fráleikrinn, en lítit ætla ek þik af honum hafa hlotit,	But though may be swiftness, but little suppose I you of it have bound-to,	But though one can still be swift, but I suppose you have little of that,
ok væria þér verri vænleikr minni, ok kæmist þú með öðrum mönnum".	and be to-you worse handsome less, and come you as other men".	and you should be less handsome, and quicker as other men are".

The Tale of Hreiðarr the Fool (Old Norse)

Old Norse	Literal	English
Þórðr svaraði:	Thord answered:	Thord answered:
"Eigi veit ek mér verr fara óknáleik minn en þér afl þitt".	"Not know I me worse to-be prowess mine than you strength yours".	"I do not know if it is worse to have my weakness than your strength".
"Handkrækjumst þá, bróðir",	"Hands-hook-us then, brother",	"Let us hook hands then, brother",
segir Hreiðarr,	said Hreidar,	said Hreidar,
ok nú gera þeir svá, fara um hríð, ok er svá, at Þórði tekr at dofna höndin, ok lætr hann laust, þykkir eigi verða vinveitt, at þeir haldist á, við álpun Hreiðars.	and now did they so, went about awhile, and was seen, that Thord took that numb hand, and had he let-go, felt not was friendly, that they rather that, against rough Hreidar.	and so they did, and after a while, and Thord's hand became so numb, that he had to let go, and he felt it was not friendly, because Hreidar was too rough.
Hreiðarr ferr nú undan svá við fót ok nemr stað síðan á hæð nökkurri ok er allstarsýnn, sér þaðan fjölmennit, þangat sem mótit var.	Hreidar went now away-from so with foot and took place afterwards to height some and was fixed-upon, saw from-there many-people, there as meeting were.	Hreidar now went away and ran, and so it happened afterwards, that he came to a hill and stopped there, he looked from there and saw many people, that were at a meeting.
Ok er Þórðr kemr eftir, mælti hann:	And as Thord came after, spoke he:	And as Thord came afterwards, he spoke:
"Förum nú báðir saman, bróðir".	"Going now both together, brother".	"Let's go both together now, brother".
Ok Hreiðarr gerir svá.	And Hreidar did so.	And Hreidar did so.

3

Ok er þeir koma á þingit, kenna margir menn Þórð ok fagna honum vel, ok verðr konungr áheyrsli.	And when they came to assembly, knew many people Thord and welcomed him well, and became the-king to-hear.	And when they came to the assembly, many people knew Thord and welcomed him well, and the king came to hear of him.
Ok þegar gengr Þórðr fyrir konung ok kveðr hann vel, ok tekr konungr blíðlíga kveðju hans.	And soon went Thord before the-king and greeted he well, and took the-king joyfully greeting his.	And soon Thord went before the king and greeted him well, and the king received his greeting joyfully.

The Tale of Hreiðarr the Fool (Old Norse)

Old Norse	Literal	English
Þegar skilði með þeim bræðrum, er þeir kómu til þingsins, ok verðr Hreiðarr skauttogaðr mjök ok færðr í reikuð.	When parted with them brothers, that they came to their-assembly, and became Hreidar roughly much and brought to roughly-handled.	When the brothers parted when they came to the assembly, Hreidar was treated roughly and pushed about.
Hann er málugr ok hlær mjök, ok þykkir mönnum ekki at minna gaman at eiga við hann, ok verðr honum nú förin ógreið.	He was talkative and laughed much, and thought people not that less fun that had with him, and became he now travelling un-passable.	He was talkative and laughed a lot, and people thought it no less fun to tease him, and he now became blocked in the crowd.
Konungr spyrr Þórð tíðenda, ok síðan spyrr hann, hvat þeira manna væri í för með honum, er hann vildi, at til hirðvistar færi með honum.	The-king asked Thord news, and then asked he, what they people were by travelling with him, that he wished, that to court-visit bring with him.	The king asked Thord for news, and then he asked, and what people were travelling with him, and whether he wished to join him at court.
"Þar er bróðir minn í för",	"There has brother mine so travelled",	"My brother has also travelled here",
segir Þórðr.	said Thord.	said Thord.
"Sá maðr mun vel vera",	"Such man should well be",	"Such a man should be well",
segir konungr, "ef þér er líkr".	said the-king, "if you is like".	said the king, "if he is like you".
Þórðr segir:	Thord said:	Thord said:
"Ekki er hann mér glíkr".	"Not is he me like".	"He is not like me".
Konungr mælti:	The-king spoke:	The king spoke:
"Þó má enn vel vera, eða hvat er ólíkast með ykkr?"	"Though may but well be, but how is unlike with you?"	"That may be, but now is he not like you?"
Þórðr mælti:	Thord spoke:	Thord spoke:
"Hann er mikill maðr vexti.	"He is great man grown.	"He is very large.
Hann er ljótr ok heldr ósýknligr, srterkr at afli ok lundhægr maðr".	He is ugly and behold un-innocent-looking, strong in strength and even-spirit man".	He is ugly, and he appears devious looking, and he is greatly strong, but even spirited".
Konungr mælti:	The-king spoke:	The king spoke:

The Tale of Hreiðarr the Fool (Old Norse)

Old Norse	Literal	English
"Þó má honum vel vera farit at mörgu".	"Though may he well be going that many-ways".	"He may be well in other ways".
Þórðr segir:	Thord said:	Thord said:
"Ekki var hann kallaðr vizkumaðr á unga aldri".	"Not was he called wise-man in young age".	"He was not called a wise man in his youth".
"At því fer ek meir",	"That then go I further",	"Then I go further",
segir konungr, "sem nú er, eða hvárt má hann sjálfr annast sik?"	said the-king, "as now to, but how may he himself take-care-of such?"	said the king, "to how he is now, and how he takes care of himself?"
"Ekki dála er þat",	"Not bad is that",	"Not bad",
segir Þórðr.	said Thord.	said Thord.
Konungr mælti:	The-king spoke:	The king spoke:
"Hví fluttir þú hann útan?"	"Why brought you him out?"	"Why did you bring him out?"
"Herra",	"Lord",	"Lord",
segir Þórðr, "hann á allt hálft við mik, en hefir engar nytjar fjárins ok engi afskipti sér veitt um penninga, beiðzt þessa eins hlutar, at fara útan með mér, ok þótti mér ósannligt, at eigi réði hann einum hlut, þars hann lætr mik mörgum ráða.	said Thord, "he has altogether half with me, but has no use of-wealth and none dealings so given about money, best this one's share, that travel out with me, and thought me untrue, that not decide he alone share, there he leaves much many advice.	said Thord, "he has half of everything with me, but he has no use of wealth and no interest in money, the only thing he has asked me is to travel abroad with me, and I thought it would be unfair to decide to leave him alone, when he lets me decide so much.
Þótti mér ok glíkligt, at hann mundi gæfu af yðr hljóta, ef hann kæmi á yðvarn fund".	Thought me and favourable, that he would be-gifted of your luck, if he came to you meet".	I thought it would be favourable and good luck if he came to meet you".
"Sjá vilda ek hann",	"So willed I him",	"So I wish to meet him",
segir konungr.	said the-king.	said the king.
"Svá skal ok",	"So shall and",	"So shall it be",
segir Þórðr, "en brottu er hann nú rjáðr nökkur".	said Thord, "but steep is he now worried somewhat".	said Thord, "but he is now somewhat worried".
Konungr sendi nú eftir honum.	The-king sent now after him.	The king now sent for him.

The Tale of Hreiðarr the Fool (Old Norse)

Old Norse	Literal	English
Ok er Hreiðarr heyrði sagt, at konungr vildi hitta hann, þá gengr hann uppstert mjök ok nær á hvat, sem fyrir var, ok var hann því óvanr, at konungr hefði beiðzt fundar hans.	And when Hreidar heard said, that the-king wished meet him, then walked he upright much and near to what, as before was, and was he then unaccustomed, to the-king having asked to-meet him.	And when Hreidar heard it said, that the king wished to meet him, then he walked very upright and near to what was before him, and he was then unaccustomed to the king having asked to meet him.
Hann var á þá leið búinn, at hann var í ökulbrókum ok hafði feld grán yfir sér.	He was that then way dressed, that he was in ankle-breeches and had cloak grey over himself.	He was dressed in such a way, that he was wearing ankle-breeches and a grey cloak over him.
Ok er hann kemr fyrir konung, þá fellr hann á kné fyrir konung ok kveðr hann Vel.	And when he came before the-king, then fell he on knees before the-king and greeted him Well.	And when he came before the king, he then fell on his knees before the king and greeted him well.
Konungr svaraði honum hlæjandi ok mælti:	The-king answered him laughing and spoke:	The king laughed and said:
"Ef þú átt við mik erendi, þá mæl þú skjótt slíkt, er þú vill.	"If you have with me business, then say you swiftly such, as you will.	"If you have business with me, then say as swiftly as you will.
Aðrir eigu enn nauðsyn at tala við mik síðan".	Others have but need to talk with me after".	There are others who need to talk with me afterwards".
Hreiðarr segir:	Hreidar said:	Hreidar said:
"Mitt erendi þykkir mér skyldast.	"My business think to-me obliged.	"I think my business is more urgent.
Ek vilda sjá þik, konungr".	I wished to-see you, king".	I wished to see you, king".
"Þykkir þér nú vel þá",	"Think you now well then",	"Do you think it well now",
segir konungr, "er þú sér mik?"	said the-king, "that you saw me?"	said the king, "that you saw me?"
"Vel víst",	"Well certainly",	"Well certainly",
segir Hreiðarr, "en eigi þykkjumst ek enn til gerla sjá þik".	said Hreidar, "but not think I that to completely saw you".	said Hreidar, "but I don't think that I have seen you completely".
"Hvernig skulum vit nú þá?"	"Which shall we now then?"	"What shall we do now then?"

The Tale of Hreiðarr the Fool (Old Norse)

Old Norse	Literal	English
segir konungr.	said the-king.	said the king.
"Vildir þú, at ek stæða upp?"	"Would you, that I stand up?"	"Would you like me to stand up?"
Hreiðarr svarar:	Hreidar answered:	Hreidar answered:
"Þat vilda ek",	"That wish i",	"That I would wish",
segir hann.	said he.	he said.
Konungr mælti, er hann var upp staðinn:	The-king spoke, then he was up standing:	The king spoke, when he stood up:
"Nú muntu þykkjast gerla sjá mik mega?"	"Now should-you consider completely seen me may?"	"Now have you seen me completely?"
"Eigi enn til gerla",	"Not then to completely",	"Not completely",
segir Hreiðarr, "ok er nú þó nær hófi".	said Hreidar, "and are now though near measure".	said Hreidar, "but it is now closer".
"Villtu þá",	"Wish-you then",	"Do you wish then",
segir konungr, "at ek leggja af mér skikkjuna?"	said the-king, "that I take off my cloak?"	said the king, "that I take off my cloak?"
"Þat vilda ek víst,	"That wish I certainly",	"That I certainly wish",
segir Hreiðarr.	said Hreidar.	said Hreidar.
Konungr mælti:	The-king spoke:	The king spoke:
"Vit skulum þar þó nökkut innast til áðr um þat málit.	"We should there though some do to before about that discuss.	"We should then discuss the matter before doing it.
Þér eruð hugkvæmir margir, Íslendingar, ok Veit ek eigi, nema þú virðir þetta til ginningar.	You are very-smart many, Icelander, and Know I not, except you worth this to mocking.	You Icelanders are very smart, and I do not know, if this is mockery.
Nú vil ek þat undan skilja".	Now wish I that away-from understand".	Now I wish to be away from that, you understand".
Hreiðarr segir:	Hreidar said:	Hreidar said:

The Tale of Hreiðarr the Fool (Old Norse)

Old Norse	Literal	English
"Engi er til þess færr, konungr, at ginna þik eða ljúga at þér".	"None that to this capable, king, of mocking you or lie to you".	"I am not capable of this, king, of mocking you or lying to you".
Konungr leggr nú af sér skikkjuna ok mælti:	The-king laid now off his cloak and spoke:	The king now took off his cloak and poke:
"Hyggðu nú at mér svá vandliga sem þik tíðir".	"Think now that me so closely as you wish".	"Think now that you may see me as closely as you wish".
"Svá skal vera",	"So shall be",	"So it shall be",
segir Hreiðarr.	said Hreidar.	said Hreidar.
Hann gengr í hring um konunginn ok mælti oft it sama fyrir munni sér:	He walked in a-ring around the-king and spoke frequently to himself before mouth his:	He walked in a ring around the king and spoke frequently to himself and mumbling:
"Allvel, allvel",	"All-well, all-well",	"Splendid, splendid",
segir hann.	said he.	he said.
Konungr mælti:	The-king spoke:	The king spoke:
"Hefir þú nú sét mik sem þú villt?"	"Have you now seen me as you wish?"	"Have you now seen me as you wish?"
"At vísu",	"That certainly",	"Certainly"
segir hann.	said he.	he said.
Konungr spurði:	The-king asked:	The king asked:
"Hversu lízt þér nú á mik þá?"	"How-so appears to-you now of me then?"	"How do I appear to you now then?"
Hreiðarr svarar:	Hreidar answered:	Hreidar answered:
"Ekki hefir Þórðr, bróðir minn, ofsögum frá þér sagt, þat er vel er".	"Not had Thord, brother mine, off-said from you said, that is well be".	"My brother Thord did not exaggerate when he said of your well being".
Konungr mælti:	The-king spoke:	The king spoke:
"Máttu nökkut at finna um þat, er þú sér nú, ok þat, er eigi sé í alþýðu viti?"	"May-you something to find about that, which you see now, and that, is not seen by all-the-people knowing?"	"Can you find something that you see now, that has not been seen by other people?"

The Tale of Hreiðarr the Fool (Old Norse)

Old Norse	Literal	English
"Ekki vil ek at finna",	"Not wish I to find",	"I do not wish to find",
segir hann, "ok ekki má ek þegar, því at þannig myndi hverr sik kjósa sem þú ert, þó at sjálfr mætti ráða".	said he, "and not may I from-there, accordingly that thus would each themselves choose as you are, though that self may advise".	he said, "and I can not find, because thus would everyone choose to be as you are, if they could".
"Mikinn tekr þú af",	"Great take you of",	"You are taking off",
segir konungr.	said the-king.	said the king.
Hreiðarr svarar:	Hreidar answered:	Hreidar answered:
"Háttung er öðrum á þá",	"Risk are others for then",	"It is a risk for others then",
segir hann, "at lofgjarnliga sé við mælt, ef þú átt þetta eigi at sönnu, sem mér lízt á þik ok ek sagða áðan".	said he, "that praise-will you of speaking, if you that this not that true, as to-me appears of you and I said earlier".	he said, "for those who praise you, if it is not true, how you appear to me as I said earlier".
Konungr mælti:	The-king spoke:	The king spoke:
"Finn til nökkut, þó at smátt sé".	"Find to something, though that small is".	"Find something, though it is small".
"Þat helzt þá, herra",	"Is rather then, lord",	"It is then rather",
segir hann, "at auga þitt annat er litlu því ofar en annat".	said he, "that eye the other is a-little before above the other".	he said, "that one eye is a little above the other".
"Þat hefir einn maðr fyrr fundit",	"That has one man before found",	"Only one man has noticed that before",
segir konungr, "en sá er Haraldr konungr, frændi minn.	said the-king, "and that was Harald the-king, kinsman mine.	said the king, "and that was King Harald, my kinsman.
Nú skal jafnmæli með okkr",	Now shall equal-speak with you",	Now I shall equally say of you",
segir konungr.	said the-king.	said the king.
"Skaltu nú standa upp ok leggja af þér skikkju, ok vil ek sjá þik".	"Shall-you now stand up and allow off your cloak, and will I see you".	"Stand up and take off your cloak, and I will see you".

The Tale of Hreiðarr the Fool (Old Norse)

Old Norse	Literal	English
Hreiðarr fleygir af sér feldinum ok hefir saurgar krummur, - maðrinn hentr mjök ok ljótr - en þvegnar heldr latliga.	Hreidar threw off his cloak and had dirty hands, a-man suited much and ugly but to-wash rather negligently.	Hreidar threw off his cloak, and he had large dirty hands, suited to such an ugly man, and washed negligently.
Konungr hyggr at honum vandliga.	The-king looked at him closely.	The king looked at him closely.
Ok þá mælir Hreiðarr:	And then spoke Hreidar:	And then Hreidar spoke:
"Herra",	"Lord",	"Lord",
segir hann, "hvat þykkist þú nú mega at mér finna?"	said he, "what think you now may that me find?"	he said, "what do you think you may find?"
Konungr segir:	The-king said:	The king said:
"Þat ætla ek, at eigi fæðist ljótari maðr upp en þú ert".	"That suppose i, that not born uglier man up than you are".	"That I suppose that there is not a man born uglier than you".
"Slíkt verðr mælt",	"Such becomes spoken",	"This is what is said",
segir Hreiðarr.	said Hreidar.	said Hreidar.
"Er nökkut þá",	"But some then",	"But are there some",
segir hann, "at til fríðenda sé um mik, at því sem þú leggr ætlan á?"	said he, "that to good-things see about me, that therefore which you have suppose of?"	he said, "good things to see about me, that you might suppose?"
Konungr mælti:	The-king spoke:	The king spoke:
"Þat sagði Þórðr, bróðir þinn, af þú værir lundhægr maðr".	"That said Thord, brother yours, of you be tempered-even man".	"That your brother Thord said you are an even-tempered man".
"Þat er satt ok",	"That is true also",	"That is also true",
sagði Hreiðarr, "ok þykkir mér þat illt, er svá er".	said Hreidar, "and think me that ill, is so to-be".	said Hreidar, "and I think that it is bad to be".
"Þú munt reiðast þó",	"Though shall-you anger though",	"Though one day you will become angry",
sagði konungr.	said the-king.	said the king.
"Mæl heill, herra",	"Say whole, lord",	"Speak well, lord",

The Tale of Hreiðarr the Fool (Old Norse)

Old Norse	Literal	English
segir Hreiðarr, "eða hvé langt mun til þess?"	said Hreidar, "but how long could until this?"	said Hreidar, "but how long could it be until this happens?"
"Eigi veit ek þat gerla",	"Not know I that completely",	"That I do not know completely",
segir konungr, "helzt á þessum vetri, at því er ek get til".	said the-king, "rather of this winter, that since that I guess to".	said the king, "rather some time this winter, if my guess is right".
Hreiðarr mælti:	Hreidar spoke:	Hreidar spoke:
"Seg heill sögu".	"Tell a-complete story".	"Tell a complete story".
Konungr mælti:	The-king spoke:	The king spoke:
"Ertu nökkut hagr?"	"Are-you of-any benefit?"	"Are you any good at anything?"
Hreiðarr segir:	Hreidar said:	Hreidar said:
"Aldrigi hefi ek reynt, má ek því eigi vita".	"Never have I tried, may I therefore not know".	"I have never tried, and therefore I do not know".
"Til þess þætti þó ekki ólíkligt",	"To this seems though not unlikely",	"It does not seem unlikely"
segir konungr.	said the-king.	said the king.
"Seg heill sögu",	"Tell the-whole story",	"Tell the whole story",
kvað Hreiðarr.	said Hreidar.	said Hreidar.
"Svá mun vera jafnt þegar, er þú segir þat.	"So should be equally then, as you say it.	"So shall it be, just as you say.
En vetrvistar þættumst ek þurfa".	And winter-provisions we-have I need".	And I need winter provisions".
Konungr sagði:	The-king said:	The king said:
"Heimil er mín umsjá.	"Home being mine about.	"My home is so about.
En betr þykkir mér þér þar vistin felld vera, er heldr er fátt manna".	But better think I you then stay shed be, where rather are few people".	But I think it better if you stay in the shed, where there are few people".

The Tale of Hreiðarr the Fool (Old Norse)

Old Norse	Literal	English
Hreiðarr svaraði:	Hreidar answered:	Hreidar answered:
"Svá er þat ok",	"So is it and",	"So it may be",
segir hann.	said he.	he said.
"En eigi mun svá mannfátt vera, at eigi komi þat þó upp, er mælt verðr, allra helzt þat, er hlægi þykkir í, en ek maðr ekki orðvarr, ok jafnan berr mér margt á góma.	"But not would so people-few be, that not come that though up, in spoken become, all rather that, is ridicule thought in, that I people not discreet, and equally carry I many about gums.	"But there would not be so few people, that none came up though, and in speaking something that is a joke, people think I am not discreet, and many people carry this about in their mouths.
Nú kann vera, at þeir reiði orð mín fyrir aðra menn ok spotti mik ok drepi þat at ferligu, er ek hefi at gamni eða mælik.	Now can be, that their anger words mine before other people and small me and kill that to monstrous, what I have been amuse or speak.	Now it may be that they angered my words before other people, and mocked me, and kill me for what I have been amused to speak.
Nú sýnist mér hitt vitrligra at vera heldr hjá þeim, er um mik hyggr, sem Þórðr er, bróðir minn, þótt þar sé heldr fjölmenni, en hinnig, þótt menn sé fáir ok sé þar engi til umbóta".	Now seems I find wisely to be rather by them, that about me think, as Thord is, brother mine, thought then be rather followers-many, that there, though people as few and as there no-one to put-right".	Now it seems to me the wiser thing to be beside those, who about me consider, such as Thord, my brother, though there are more people there than otherwise and there is no one to put things right".
Konungr mælti:	The-king spoke:	The king spoke:
"Ráð þú þá, ok farið báðir bræðr til hirðarinnar, ef ykkr líkar þat betr".	"Decide you then, and go both brothers to court, if you like that better".	"You decide then, and you and your brother can both come to court if you would like that better".
Þegar hljóp Hreiðarr á brott, er hann heyrði þessi orð konungs", ok segir hverjum manni, er á vill hlýða, at hans för hefir allgóð orðit á konungs fund, segir ok einkum Þórði, bróður sínum, at konungr hefir leyft honum at fara til hirðvistar.	Straightaway ran Hreidar to away, that he heard these words the-king's, and told each of-the-people, that from well listened, that his going had all-good words from the-king visit, said and especially Thord, brother his, that the-king had given-leave him to travel to court.	Then Hreidar ran away when he heard the king's words, and told every person who listened, how it had gone with all the good words from his visit to the king, and said especially to his brother Thord, that the king had given them leave to travel to court.
Þá mælti Þórðr:	Then spoke Thord:	Then Thord spoke:

The Tale of Hreiðarr the Fool (Old Norse)

Old Norse	Literal	English
"Bú þik þá sæmiliga at klæðum eða vápnum, því at þ-at eitt samir, ok skortir okkr ekki til þess, ok skipast margir menn vel við góðan búning, enda er vandara at búa sik í konungs herbergi en annars staðar, ok verðr síðr at hlægi gerr af hirðmönnum".	"Prepare you then well-enough with clothes and weapons, because that it one in-common, and shortage ours not to this, and changed many people well with good clothing, and is important to dress such as the-king's room than any-other place, and become less the ridicule made of court-men".	"Prepare yourself well with clothes and weapons, because there is one thing in common, and we have no shortage in this, and many people are changed by good clothing, and it is important to dress well in the king's room more than any other place, and it will avoid ridicule from the court-men".
Hreiðarr svarar:	Hreidar answered:	Hreidar answered:
"Eigi getr þú allnær, at ek muna skrúðklæðin á mik láta koma".	"Not get you all-near, that I should costly-clothing of me allow coming".	"You will not get anywhere near me coming along wearing fancy clothing".
Þórðr mælti:	Thord spoke:	Thord spoke:
"Skerum vaðmál þá til".	"Cut homespun-cloth then to".	"Then you will wear cut homespun cloth".
Hreiðarr svarar:	Hreidar answered:	Hreidar answered:
"Nær er þat",	"Near is that",	"That would be better",
segir hann.	said he.	he said.
Svá er nú gert við ráð Þórðar, ok lætr Hreiðarr eftir leiðast.	So that now did with advice Thord's, and had Hreidar afterwards carried-out.	So now it was done with Thord's advice, and then Hreidar had carried it out.
Hefir hann nú vaðmálsklæði ok fágar sik ok þykkir nú þegar allr annarr maðr, sýnist nú maðr ljótr ok greitt vaskligr.	Had he now wadding-clothes and cleaned himself and seemed now already all another man, seemed now a-man ugly and ready-to-serve valiant.	Now he had wadding-clothes and cleaned himself, and he already seemed like a different man, he was still ugly, but now valiant looking.
Svá er þó mót á manninum, er þeir Þórðr eru með hirðinni, at Hreiðarr verðr í fyrstu fyrir miklum ágang af hirðmönnum, ok breyttu þeir marga vega orðum við hann ok fundu, at hann var ómállatr.	So was though against about the-people, that they Thord were with court-men, that Hreidar became the first before much aggression of court-men, and varied they many ways words with him and found, that he was talkative.	So it was though, in meeting the people, that with Thord and with the court-men, that Hreidar became singled out for much aggression from the court-me, and there were many ways in which they had words with him, and he was talkative.

The Tale of Hreiðarr the Fool (Old Norse)

Old Norse	Literal	English
Kom við sem mátti, ok hendu þeir mikit gaman at því at eiga við hann, ok var hann jafnan hlæjandi við því, er þeir mæltu, ok lagði hvern þeira fyrir, svá var hann leikmikill, bæði um mælgina ok allra helzt - -	Came with how it-may, and handed they much fun that because that had with he, and was he equally laughing with such, that they spoke, and had each they before, so was he playful, both about talking and all rather	It became how it may, that they had much fun with him, and he was laughing equally as much with them, with what they said, and with each of them he was playful, both in talking and rather in all things.
En fyrir því, at hann var rammi at afli ok er þeir finna, at hann gefst ekki at grandi, þá þvarr þat allt af þeim hirðmönnum - - [nú með] hirðinni.	When for then, that he was frame that strength and when they found, that he gave not to injury, then decreased that all of them court-men [now with] court.	Then when they realised how strong his frame was, and when they found that he did not give in to injury, then the mocking of him decreased with all the court-men.

4

Old Norse	Literal	English
Í þetta mund váru þeir báðir konungar yfir landi, Magnús konungr ok Haraldr konungr.	In that time were they both kings over the-land, Magnús the-king and Harald the-king.	At that time there were two kings ruling over the land, King Magnus, and King Harald.
En þá höfðu sakar gerzt - - hirðmaðr Magnúss konungs hafði vegit hirðmann Haralds konungs, ok var lagðr til sáttarfundr, at konungar skyldi [sjálfir finnast] ok skipa málinu.	But then had conviction made court-man Magnus's the-king had slain court-man Harald's the-king, and was laid to peace-meeting, that kings should [themselves meet-up] and exchange the-matter.	But then trouble came when one of Magnus's court-men had slain one of Harald's court-men, and they had a peace meeting, so that the kings themselves could meet up and discuss the matter.
Ok er Hreiðarr heyrir þetta, at Magnús konungr skal fara til móts við Harald konung, þá ferr hann á fund Magnúss konungs ok mælti:	And when Hreidar heard this, that Magnus the-king shall travel to meet with Harald the-king, then went he to find Magnus the-king and spoke:	And when Hreidar heard this, that King Magnus would travel to meet with King Harald, then he went to find King Magnus and spoke:
"Sá hlutr er",	"So share i",	"So I share",
segir hann, "er ek Vilda þik biðja".	said he, "that I Wish you to-ask".	he said, "something that I wish to ask you".
"Hverr er sá?"	"What is so?"	"What is it?"
sagði konungr.	said the-king.	said the king.
Hreiðarr mælti:	Hreidar spoke:	Hreidar spoke:
"At fara til sáttarfundar.	"To travel to peace-meeting.	"To travel to the peace meeting.

The Tale of Hreiðarr the Fool (Old Norse)

Old Norse	Literal	English
Em ek ekki víðförull, en mér er mikil forvitni á at sjá tvá konunga senn í einum stað".	Am I not widely-travelled, but I am much curious about to see two kings they in one place".	I am not widely travelled, but I am very curious to see two kings in one place".
Konungr svarar:	The-king answered:	The king answered:
"Satt segir þú, at þú ert ekki víðförull.	"True say you, that you are not widely-travelled.	"It is true to say that you are not widely travelled.
En þeygi mun ek leyfa þér þessa förna, því at ekki er þér fellt at ganga í greipr mönnum Haralds konungs.	But yet-not could I allow you this sacrificing, for that not are you falling to go in grasp people Harald's the-king.	But I could not allow this, to sacrifice you, if you fall into the grasp of King Harald.
Ok beri svá til, at þér verði at því ólið eða öðrum ok, em ek um þat hræddr, at þá sæki þik heim reiðin, er þú langar til, en mér þætti bezt, at við bærist".	And bear so to, that you became that for unaccompanied or others and, am I about that worried, that then conviction you home uproar, that you long to, then me seems best, that with bearing".	And so it carries, that if you become separated from the others, I am worried that, then you might be involved in trouble, and then you would become angry, and so it seems best to me, with that in mind".
Hreiðarr svarar:	Hreidar answered:	Hreidar answered:
"Nú mæltir þú gott orð.	"Now speak you good words.	"Now you speak good words.
Þá skal at vísu fara, ef ek veit þess vánir, at ek reiðumst".	Then shall to certainly travel, if I know this custom, that I become-angry".	Then I am more certain to travel, if I know that I am accustomed to becoming angry".
Konungr segir:	The-king said:	The king said:
"Muntu fara, ef ek leyfi eigi?"	"Shall-you travel, if I leave not?"	"Will you travel, if I do not give leave for it?"
Hreiðarr svarar:	Hreidar answered:	Hreidar answered:
"Eigi þá síðr".	"None then less".	"None the less".
"Ætlar þú, at þér muni þvílíkt við mik at eiga sem við Þórð, bróður þinn, því at þar hefir þú jafnan þitt mál?"	"Suppose you, that you would therefore-like with me that have as with Thord, brother yours, because that there have you always your way?"	"Do you suppose, that you would therefore liken me to that which you have with your brother Thord, because you always have your way?"

The Tale of Hreiðarr the Fool (Old Norse)

Old Norse	Literal	English
Hreiðarr segir:	Hreidar said:	Hreidar said:
"Því öllu betra mun mér við yðr at eiga sem þú ert vitrari en hann".	"Because all better would me with you than have as you are wiser than he".	"It would be better with you than with him as you are wiser than he is".
Konungr sér nú, at hann mun fara, þó at hann banni eða hann fari eigi í hans föruneyti, ok þykkir eigi þat bezt, ef hann kemr annars staðar til föruneytis, ok þykkir þá í reiðingum vera, hversu honum eirir, ef hann vælir einn um, ok leyfir honum nú heldr at fara með sér, ok er Hreiðari fenginn hestr til reiðar.	The-king saw now, that he would travel, though that he banned either he travelled not in his companionship, and thought not that best, if he came another's place to company, and thought then in uproar being, how-so he own, if he wilful one about, and leave him now rather that travel with him, and was Hreidar given a-horse to ride.	The king saw now that he would travel, even though he had banned him, he would travel outside of his companionship, and he thought it not best if he came into another place's company and there was an uproar, how he would be if he was wilful about something, and had him rather travelling with him, and Hreidar was given a horse to ride.
Ok þegar er þeir váru á ferð komnir, þá reið hann mjök ok ætlaði sér varla hóf um, ok þraut hestinn undir honum.	And as-soon as they were to travel coming, then rode he much and intended himself hardly in-moderation about, and faltered the-horse under him.	And as soon as they were coming to travel, then he rode hard, and hardly in moderation about, and the horse faltered under him.
Ok er konungr verðr þess varr, mælti hann:	And when the-king became this aware, spoke he:	And when the king became aware of this, he spoke:
"Nú gefr vel til.	"Now give well to.	"Now it is well.
Fylgið nú Hreiðari heim, ok fari hann eigi".	Follow now Hreidar home, and travel he not".	Hreidar is to be followed home and he is not to travel".
Hann segir:	He said:	"He said:
"Eigi heftir þetta ferðina mína, þótt hestrinn sé þrotinn.	"Not have this travelling mine, thought horse's being ended.	"Not having this my journey, though the horse has given out".
Kemr mér til lítils fráleikrinn, ef ek fæ eigi fylgt yðr".	Came me to little game, if I give not follow you".	I would not be a good sportsman, if I could not keep up with you".
Fara þeir nú, ok lögðu margir fram hjá honum hesta sína ok þótti gaman at reyna fráleik hans, svá gropasamliga sem hann sjálfr tók á.	Travelled they now, and had many from beside him horse his and thought fun to test from-game his, so grouped-together as he himself took of.	Travelled they now and many brought their horses beside his and thought it fun to test his sport. And so grouped together as he took them on.

The Tale of Hreiðarr the Fool (Old Norse)

Old Norse	Literal	English
En svá gafst, at hann þreytti hvern hest, er frammi var lagðr, ok lézt eigi verðr at koma til fundarins, ef hann gæti eigi fylgt þeim.	But so gave, that he tired each horse, that from was had, and let not were to come to the-meeting, if he got not follow them.	But it so happened that he tired each horse, that was laid before him, and he was not to come to the meeting if he could not follow pace with them.
Ok fyrir þetta sátu nú margir af sínum hestum.	And ahead that sat now many of his horses.	And for this many of their horses now sat.

5

Old Norse	Literal	English
Ok er þeir koma þar, er konungar skulu finnast, þá mælti Magnús konungr við Hreiðar:	And when they came there, that the-kings shall meet, then spoke Magnus the-king with Hreidar:	And when they came to where the kings were to meet, then King Magnus said to Hreidar:
"Ver þú mér nú fylgjusamr ok ver á aðra hönd mér ok skilst ekki frá mér.	"Be you me now follow-same and be on other hand mine and separate not from me.	"Be obedient to me now and me on my other side and do not part with me"
En miðlungi segir mér hugr um, hversu ferr, þá er menn Haralds konungs koma ok sjá þik".	But poorly say me think about, how-so goes, then when men Harald's the-king come and see you".	But I think that it will go badly, when King Harald's men come and see you".
Hreiðarr kvað svá vera skyldu sem konungr mælti, "ok þykkir mér því betr er ek geng yðr nær".	Hreidar spoke so be should as the-king spoke, "and think me then better that I go you near".	Hreidar said that it should be as the king said, "and then I think it better that I go nearer to you".
Nú finnast konungar, ok ganga þeir á tal ok ræða mál sín.	Now met the-kings, and went they to talk and discuss matters theirs.	Now the kings met, and they talked and discussed their matters.
En menn Haralds konungs gátu líta, hvar Hreiðarr gekk, ok höfðu heyrt getit hans, ok þótti þeim um it vænsta.	When men Harald's the-king got company, where Hreidar went, and had heard told he, and thought they about that good.	But King Harold's men could see where Hreidar went, and they had heard his name, and they thought it good.
Ok er konungar töluðu, þá gengr Hreiðarr í flokk Haralds manna, ok höfðu þeir hann til skógar, er skammt var þaðan, skauttoguðu hann mjök ok hrundu honum stundum.	And as the-kings talked, then went Hreidar in group Harald's men, and had they he to woods, which short-distance was from-there, pull-cloak, handle-roughly he much and teased him awhile.	And when the kings were talking, Hreidar went into the company of Harold's men, and they took him to a forest, which was not far from there, they rough-handled him a lot, and sometimes knocked him down.

The Tale of Hreiðarr the Fool (Old Norse)

Old Norse	Literal	English
En þar lék á ýmsu.	But then played about variously.	But they played at him in various ways.
Stundum fauk hann fyrir sem vindli, en stundum var hann fastr fyrir sem veggr, ok hrutu þeir frá honum.	Sometimes drifted he before as wind, then sometimes was he secure before as a-wall, and fell they away-from him.	Sometimes he drifted before them like the wind, and sometimes he was as secure as a wall, and they fell away from him.
Nú dregst þó svá leikrinn, at þeir gera honum nökkut harðleikit, létu ganga honum öxarsköft ok skálpana, ok námu naddar af sverðskónum í höfði honum, ok skeindist hann af, ok svá lét hann sem honum þætti it mesta gaman at ok hló við jafnan.	Now drawn though so the-game, that they did him some hardness, had going him axe-handles and scabbards, and took studded of sword-studded at head him, and scratched he of, and so had he as him seemed the most game that and laughed with equally.	And as the game drew on, they became hard and were going at him with axe handles and scabbards, and a studded sword scabbard hit him on the head, and scratched him, and he appeared to enjoy the game and laughed equally with them.
Ok er svá hafði fram farit um hríð, þá tók leikrinn ekki at batna af þeira hendi.	And was so had from going about awhile, then took the-game not to better of them hand.	And when this had been going on for a while, the game did not begin to get any better from them.
Þá mælti Hreiðarr:	Then spoke Hreidar:	Then Hreidar spoke:
"Nú höfum vér átt góðan leik um stund, ok er nú ráð at hætta, því at nú tekr mér at leiðast.	"Now have we had good sport about awhile, and am-i now decide that conclude, therefore that now take me to hand.	"How we have had good sport for a while, and I have now decided that it shall conclude, therefore take my hand.
Förum nú til konungs yðvars, ok vil ek sjá hann".	Go now to king yours, and will I see him".	Let's go now to your king, and I will see him.
"Þat skal verða aldri",	"That shall be never",	"That shall never be",
sögðu þeir, "svá fjandligr sem þú ert, at þú skulir sjá konung várn, ok skulum vér færa þik til heljar".	said they, "so fiendish as you are, that you should see the-king ours, and shall we bring you to death".	they said, "so fiendish as you are, that you should see our king, and we shall bring you to death".

The Tale of Hreiðarr the Fool (Old Norse)

Old Norse	Literal	English
Honum finnst þá fátt um ok þykkist sjá, at þat mun fram fara, ok er nú þar komit, at honum rennr í skap, ok reiðist hann, ferr höndum þann mann, er mest sótti at honum ok verst lék við hann, ok vegr á loft ok færði niðr at höfðinu, svá at heilinn var úti, ok er sá dauðr.	He found then little about and thought seemed, that it would from go, and that now there came, that he run of mood, and angered he, went seized then man, the most took with him and worse played with he, and proceeded to lift and brought down on head, so that brain was out, and was so dead.	He found that he did not like this at all, and where it seemed it would go, and then it happened, that his mood changed, and he became very angry, he seized the man who had taunted him the worst, and proceeded to lift him up and bring him down on his head, so that his brains came out, and he was dead.
Nú þykkir þeim hann trautt mennskr maðr at afli, ok stukku þeir nú í víginu, fara ok segja Haraldi konungi, at drepinn var hirðmaðr hans.	Now thought they he scarcely human man that strength, and leapt they now from the-slaying, went and told Harald the-king, that killed was court-man his.	Now they thought that he was scarcely human with that strength, and they leapt away from the slaying and told King Harald, that one of his court-men had been killed.
Konungr svarar:	The-king answered:	The king answered:
"Drepið þann þá, er þat hefir unnit".	"Kill he then, who this has done".	"Kill him then, the one who has done this".
"Eigi er þat enn hægra",	"Not is that then easy",	"That is not easy",
segja þeir.	said they.	they said.
"Hann er nú í brottu".	"He is now to away".	"He has now gone away".
Þat er nú frá Hreiðari at segja, at hann hittir Magnús konung.	That is now from Hreidar to say, that he found Magnus the-king.	It is now said of Hreidar that he met King Magnus.
Konungr mælti:	The-king spoke:	The king spoke:
"Veiztu nú, hvernig þat er at reiðast?"	"Know-you now, how that is that anger?"	"Now do you know how your anger is?"
"Já",	"Yes",	"Yes",
segir hann, "nú veit ek".	said he, "now know i".	he said, "now I know".
"Hvernig þótti þér?"	"How thought you?"	"What did you think of it?"
segir konungr.	said the-king.	said the king?
"Hitt fann ek, at þér var forvitni á".	"It found i, that you were curious to".	"I found it that you were curious about it".

The Tale of Hreiðarr the Fool (Old Norse)

Old Norse	Literal	English
Hreiðarr svarar:	Hreidar answered:	Hreidar answered:
"Illt þótti mér.	"Badly thought i.	"I thought it bad.
Þess var ek fúsastr at drepa þá alla".	This was I wished to kill then all".	This was my wish, to then kill them all".
Konungr mælti:	The-king spoke:	The king spoke:
"Þat kom mér jafnt í hug",	"That came to-me equally in thought",	"The same thing came to my thoughts",
segir konungr, "at þú myndir illa reiðr verða.	said the-king, "that you would badly angry become.	said the king, "that you would become bad when angry.
Nú vil ek senda þik á Upplönd til Eyvindar, lends manns míns, at hann haldi þik fyrir Haraldi konungi.	Now will I send you to Uplands to Eyvind, land man mine, that he hold you from Harald the-king.	Now I will send you to Uplands to Eyvind, a land man of mine, so that he protects you from King Harald.
Því at ek treystumst eigi, at þín verði gætt, ef þú ert með hirðinni, því at vér finnumst, en Haraldr frændi er brögðóttr, ok er vant við at sjá.	Because that I we-trust not, that you become taken-care-of, if you are with court-men, because that we find, that Harald's kinsmen are tricky, and are difficult with to see.	I do not trust that you will be taken care of if you are with the court-men, because we find Harald's kinsmen are tricky, and difficult to see.
Kom þá aftr til mín, er ek sendi eftir þér".	Come then back to me, when I send after you".	Then come back to me, when I send for you".
Nú ferr Hreiðarr í brott, unz hann kemr á Upplönd, ok tekr Eyvindr við honum eftir orðsending konungs.	Now went Hreidar to away, until he came to Uplands, and took Eyvind with him after message the-king's.	Now Hreidar went away, until he came to Uplands, and Eyvind received him as per the king's message.
Konungar höfðu sáttir orðit á þat mál, er áðr var milli þeira, ok var því sætt.	The-kings had agreed words of the matter, that before was between them, and was therefore settled.	The kings had agreed words about the matter, which was between them, and it was therefore settled.
En hér verða þeir eigi á sáttir.	But here became they not about agreed.	But here they became not in agreement.

The Tale of Hreiðarr the Fool (Old Norse)

Old Norse	Literal	English
Þykkir Magnúsi þessir menn hafa sjálfir fyrirgert sér ok valdit öllum sökum ok þykkir hirðmaðr fallit hafa óheilagr.	Thought Magnus these men had themselves fore-done him and wielded all blame and thought court-man fallen had unholy.	Magnus thought that these men had forgiven themselves and wielded all the blame, and thought that the court-man had fallen unholy.
En Haraldr konungr beiðir bóta fyrir hirðmann ísinn, ok skilðust nú með engri sætt.	Then Harald the-king asked compensation for court-man his, and separated now with no settlement.	But King Harald begged compensation for his court-man, and now they parted with no settlement.

6

Old Norse	Literal	English
Eigi liðu langar stundir, áðr Haraldr konungr spyrr, hvar Hreiðarr er niðr kominn, gerir síðan ferð sína ok kemr á Upplönd til Eyvindar, hefir með sér sex tigu manna.	Not passed long while, before Harald the-king learned, where Hreidar then down came, made afterwards travelled he and came to Uplands to Eyvind, had with him six tens men.	Not a long while had passed, before King Harald learned where Hreidar had come down to, and went afterwards to travel and come to Uplands to Eyvind, having with him sixty men.
Hann kemr þar um morgin snemma ok ætlaði at koma á óvart.	He came there about morning early and intended to come to un-warned.	He came there early in the morning and intended to come without warning.
En þat var þó eigi, því at Eyvindr þóttist vita fyrir, at hann myndi koma, ok var hann á engri stundu vanbúinn við.	But that was though not, therefore that Eyvind thought knowing before, that he would come, and was he that no time unprepared against.	But that was not to be, because Eyvind had thought before that he knew that he would come, and at no time was he unprepared against this.
Hafði hann stefnt liði at sér af launungu, ok var þat í skógum þeim, er nálægir váru bænum.	Had he located company that he of secretly, and was that in the-woods they, were near-lying were dwelling.	He had located a company secretly, and they were in the woods, lying near the dwelling.
Skyldi Eyvindr gefa þeim mark, ef Haraldr konungr kæmi, ok þættist hann liðs þurfa.	Should Eyvind give them sign, if Harald the-king came, and thought he company needed.	And Eyvind was to give them a sign, if King Harald came, and if he thought he needed company.
Þat er sagt, einhverju sinni, áðr Haraldr konungr kæmi, at Hreiðarr beiddist, at Eyvindr skyldi fá honum silfr ok nökkut gull.	It was said, once this, after Harald the-king came, that Hreidar asked, that Eyvind should get him silver and some gold.	It was said that once King Harald had arrived, Hreidar asked Eyvind to get him silver and some gold.
"Ertu hagr?"	"Are-you handy?"	"Are you handy?"

The Tale of Hreiðarr the Fool (Old Norse)

Old Norse	Literal	English
segir hann..	said he.	he said.
Hreiðarr svarar:	Hreidar answered:	Hreidar answered:
"Þat sagði Magnús konungr mér.	"That said Magnus the-king to-me.	"King Magnus said that to me.
En eigi má ek annat til vita, því at ek hefi aldri við leitat.	But not may I other to know, because that I have never with sought.	But I must know nothing else, for I have never sought.
En því myndi hann þat segja, at hann myndi vita, ok því trúi ek, er hann sagði".	But because should he that say, that he would know, and therefore trust i, what he said".	But because he said that, he should know, and therefore I trust what he said".
Eyvindr mælti:	Eyvind spoke:	Eyvind spoke:
"Þú ert undarligr maðr",	"You are a-strange man",	"You are a strange man",
segir hann.	said he.	he said.
"Nú mun ek fá þér efnin.	"Now should I give you materials.	"Now should I get you the materials.
Skaltu fá mér silfrit, ef ónýtt verðr smíðat, en njót sjálfr elligar".	Shall-you get me silver, if ruined becomes made, then enjoy yourself otherwise".	You shall get silver from me, but if the construction becomes ruined, give it back to me, if not, enjoy yourself".
Hreiðarr er byrgðr í einu húsi, ok er hann þar at smíðinni.	Hreidar then closed in a house, and was he there to smith.	Hreidar was then kept in a house, and he began there his smithery.
Ok áðr en gert verði þat, er Hreiðarr smíðaði, þá kemr Haraldr konungr, ok er nú sem ek gat áðr, at Eyvindr er at engu óbúinn, ok gerir hann konungi veizlu góða.	And before then made was that, which Hreidar making, then came Harald the-king, and was now as I got before, that Eyvind was that none unprepared, and made he the-king feast good.	And before Hreidar finished what he was making, then came King Harald, and it was now as said before, that Eyvind was not unprepared, and he made the king a good feast.
Ok nú er þeir sitja í drykkju, þá fréttir konungr eftir, ef Hreiðarr sé þar, - ok muntu hafa vináttu af mér í móti, ef þú selr oss manninn".	And now were they sitting to drinking, then news the-king afterwards, of Hreidar seeing there, and shall-you have friendship of me in meeting, if you sell us the-man".	And now when they were sitting drinking, then the King heard that Hreidar had been seen there, "and you shall have my friendship meeting if you sell us the man".
Eyvindr svarar:	Eyvind answered:	Eyvind answered:

The Tale of Hreiðarr the Fool (Old Norse)

Old Norse	Literal	English
"Eigi er hann hér nú".	"Not is he here now".	"He is not here now".
"Ek veit",	"I know",	"I know",
segir konungr, "at hann er, ok þarftu eigi dylja".	said the-king, "that he is, and need-you not disguise".	said the king, "that he is, and you need not disguise it".
Eyvindr mælti:	Eyvind spoke:	Eyvind spoke:
"Enn þótt þat sé, þá geri ek eigi þann mun ykkar Magnúss konungs, at ek selja þann mann í hendr þér, er hann vill skýla láta", - gekk út síðan ór stofunni.	"But though that he, then do I not then would you Magnus the-king, that I sell then that-man in hand you, then he will protect be", went out afterwards out-of the-room.	"Even though he is, then I would not then betray King Magnus by selling that man to you and handing over the man he wishes to be protected", and with that he went out of the room.
Ok er hann kemr út, þá brýzt Hreiðarr á hurðina ok kallar, at hann vill á brott.	And when he came out, then hammering Hreidar to the-door and called, that he wished to away.	And when he came out, then Hreidar began hammering on the door and calling that he wished to get out.
"Þegi þú",	"Silent you",	"Be quiet"
segir Eyvindr.	said Eyvind.	said Eyvind.
"Haraldr konungr er hér kominn ok vill drepa þik".	"Harald the-king is here come and wishes to-kill you".	"King Harald has come here and he wishes to kill you".
Hreiðarr brýzt út eigi at síðr ok lézt hitta vildu konung.	Hreidar hammering out not the less and let meet wiled the-king.	Hreidar hammered on the door no less, and wished to meet the king.
Eyvindr sér þá, at hann mun brjóta upp hurðina, gengr til ok lýkr upp ok mælir:	Eyvind himself then, that he would break up the-door, going to and concluded up and spoke:	Eyvind saw then that he was going to break open the door, and went and unlocked it and said:
"Gramir munu taka þik",	"Anger shall take you",	"Anger shall take you",
segir hann, "er þú gengr til banans".	said he, "then you go to death".	he said, "then you go to your death".

The Tale of Hreiðarr the Fool (Old Norse)

Old Norse	Literal	English
Hreiðarr gengr inn í stofuna ok fyrir konung ok kveðr hann ok mælti:	Hreidar went in to the-room and before the-king and spoke he and said:	Hreidar went into the room and before the king and spoke to him and said:
"Herra, tak af mér reiðina, því at ek em þér vel felldr fyrir margs sakar at gera þat, er þú vill gera láta, þó at eigi sé allrífligt, í mannraunum eða því, er við berr, ok mun ek þess ólatr, er þú vill mik til hafa sendan.	"Lord, take off me anger, because that I am to-you well situated for many reasons to do that, which you wish done have, though that not is all-abundant, in human-trials or otherwise, is with carrying, and should I this not-forget, when you wish me to have sent.	"Lord, do not be angry with me, because I am pleased to do that which you wish to have done, even though it may not seem rich in human trials or so carried with, and I will not forget it, when you will have me sent for.
Hér er nú gripr, er ek vil gefa þér", - setr á borðit fyrir hann, en þat var svín, gert af silfri ok gyllt.	Here is now treasure, that I wish to-give you", set on table before him, then that was a-pig, made of silver and gold.	Here is now a treasure, that I wish to give you", he set it on the table before him, and it was a pig made of silver and gold.
Þá mælti konungr, er hann leit á svínit:	Then spoke the-king, that he looked at the-pig:	Then the king spoke when he looked at the-pig:
"Þú ert hagr, svá at trautt hefi ek sét jafnvel smíðat með því móti, sem er".	"You are skilled, so that scarcely have I seen equally-well smithery with this of, such as".	"You are so skilled, that scarcely have I seen such craftsmanship as this".
Nú ferr þat með manna höndum.	Now passed that among the-men handed.	Now it passed among people's hands.
Segir konungr, at hann mun taka sættir af honum, - "ok er gott at senda þik til stórvirkja.	Said the-king, that he would take settle of him, "and was god that sending you to great-work.	The king said that he would he would take settlement with him, "and it would be good to send you on great work.
Þú ert maðr sterkr ok ófælinn, at því er ek hygg".	You are a-man strong and without-fear, that therefore am I minded".	You are a strong man and without fear, and therefore I am minded".
Nú kemr svínit aftr fyrir konung.	Now came the-pig before in-front-of the-king.	Now came the pig back to the king.
Tekr hann þá upp ok hyggr at smíðinni enn vandligar ok sér þá, at spenar eru á ok þat var gyltr, fleygir þegar í brott ok sér, at til háðs var gert, ok mælti:	Took he then up and considered that the-work then carefully and saw then, that suckling was then and that was young-sow, threw then to away and he, that to mockery was done, and spoke:	He then picked it up and looked at the work then carefully, and then he saw that the pig was a suckling and a young-sow, then he threw it away, because he believed that it insulted him, and he spoke:

The Tale of Hreiðarr the Fool (Old Norse)

Old Norse	Literal	English
"Hafi þik allan tröll.	"Have you all monstrous.	"Have you all, the devil.
Standi menn upp ok drepi hann".	Stand men up and kill him".	Stand up men and kill him".
En Hreiðarr tekr svínit ok gengr út ok ferr þegar á brott þaðan, korn á fund Magnúss konungs ok segir honum, hvat í hefir gerzt.	Then Hreidar took the-pig and went away and travelled straightaway to away from-there, came to meet Magnus the-king and told him, what so had done.	Then Hreidar took the pig, went away and travelled straightaway from there to meet King Magnus and told him how it had gone.
En í öðru lagi standa menn upp ok út eftir honum ok ætla at drepa hann.	Then with others lead standing men up and out after him and intended to kill him.	Then the others stood up and went out after him intending to kill him.
Ok er þeir koma út, þá er Eyvindr þar fyrir ok hefir fjölmenni mikit, svá at ekki máttu þeir eftir Hreiðari halda, ok skilja þeir Eyvindr ok Haraldr konungr við svá búit, ok líkar konungi illa.	And when they came out, then was Eyvind there before and had followers many, so that not may they after Hreidar held, and parted they Eyvind and Harald the-king with so settled, and liked the-king badly.	And when they came outside, then Eyvind was there with many followers, so they could not go after Hreidar. Then Eyvind and King Harald parted, and the king was far from pleased.
Ok er þeir hittast., Magnús konungr ok Hreiðarr, fréttir konungr eftir, hvernig farit hefir.	And when they met, Magnus the-king and Hreidar, news the-king after, how fared had.	And when they met, King Magnus and Hreidar, the king asked for news of how it had gone.
En Hreiðarr segir frá it sanna ok sýndi konungi svínit.	Then Hreidar told from the truth and showed the-king the-pig.	Then Hreidar told the truth about what happened and showed the king the pig.
Magnús konungr mælti, þá er hann hugði at svíninu:	Magnus the-king spoke, then that he thought that the-pig:	King Magnus then spoke and said that he thought that the pig was:
"Geysihagliga er þetta smíðat.	"Exceedingly-skilful was that crafted.	"Exceedingly skilfully crafted.
En hefnt hefir Haraldr konungr, frændi várr, mjök minni háðungar en í þessu er, ok eigi ertu alláræðislítill ok þó með öllu hugkvæmr".	But revenge had Harald the-king, kinsman ours, much less insult than in this has, and not are-you very-timid and though with all ingenuity".	But King Harald, our kinsman, had revenge for much less of an insult than this, and you are not at all timid and though you are full of ingenuity".

The Tale of Hreiðarr the Fool (Old Norse)

Old Norse	Literal	English
7	**7**	**7**
Hreiðarr var nú þar nökkura stund með Magnúsi konungi.	Hreidar was now there some time with Magnus the-king.	Hreidar was now there some time with Magnus the-king.
Ok eitthvert sinn kemr hann at máli við konung ok mælti:	And one occasion came he to speak with the-king and spoke:	And on one occasion he came to speak with the king and said:
"Þat vilda ek, konungr, at þú veittir mér þat, er ek mun biðja þik".	"It wish I, king, that you grant me that, which I may ask you".	"It is my wish, king, that you grant me that which I ask you".
"Hvat er þat?"	"What is that?"	"What is that?"
spyrr konungr.	asked the-king.	asked the-king.
"Þat, herra",	"That, lord",	"That, lord",
segir Hreiðarr, "at þér hlýddið kvæði, er ek hefi ort um yðr".	said Hreidar, "that you listen-to poem, that I have worded about you".	said Hreidar, "that you listen-to poem, that I have worded about you".
"Hví skal eigi þat?"	"Why should not that?"	"Why should not that?"
segir konungr.	said the-king.	said the-king.
Nú kveðr Hreiðarr kvæðit, ok er þat allundarligt, fyrst kynligast, en því betra er síðar er.	Now recited Hreidar the-poem, and was it all-wonderful, first strangely, then since better then afterwards was.	Now Hreidar recited the poem, and it was all wonderful, strange at first, but then it got better after that.
Ok er lokit er kvæði, mælti konungr:	And when ended was the-poem, spoke the-king:	And when the poem had ended, the king spoke:
"Þetta kvæði sýnist mér undarligt ok þó gott at nestlokum.	"That poem seems to-me wonderful and though good as the-end.	"That poem seems to be to be wonderful, particularly good at the end.
En kvæðit mun vera með þeim hætti sem ævi þín.	Then poem should be with the way as life yours.	Then the poem should be the same way as your life.
Hon hefir fyrst verit með kynligu móti ok einrænligu, en hon mun þó vera því betr er meir líðr á.	It has first been with strange meeting and eccentric, but it shall though become therefore better the more passes so.	First it has been strange and eccentric, but it shall become better the more passes.

The Tale of Hreiðarr the Fool (Old Norse)

Old Norse	Literal	English
Hér eftir skal ek ok velja kvæðislaunin.	Here after shall I and will poem-reward.	Here after I shall give you a poem's reward.
Hér er hólmr einn fyrir Nóregi, sá er ek vil þér gefa.	Here is small-island one along Norway, so that I will you give.	Here is a small island along Norway, so I will give it to you.
Hann er með góðum grösum, ok er þat gott land, þó at eigi sé mikit".	It is with good grass, and is that good land, though is not so large".	It is good with grass, and good land, though it is not so large".
Hreiðarr mælti:	Hreidar spoke:	Hreidar spoke:
"Þar skal ek samtengja með Nóreg ok Ísland".	"There shall I unite with Norway and Iceland".	"There shall I unite with Norway and Iceland".
Konungr mælti:	The-king spoke:	The king spoke:
"Eigi veit ek, hversu þat ferr.	"One-thing know i, how-so that goes.	"I know one thing about how it goes.
Hitt veit ek, at margir menn munu búnir at kaupa at þér hólminn ok gefa þér fé fyrir.	This know i, that many people shall offer to buy of you the-island and give you fee for.	This I know, that many people shall offer to buy the island from you and give you wealth for.
En ráðligra ætla ek vera, at ek leysa til mín, at eigi verði at bitbeini þér eða þeim, er kaupa vilja.	But advisable suppose I be, that I redeem to me, that not becomes a bite-bone to-you or they, who buy wish-to.	But. I advise you to sell the island to me, so that it does not become a bone of contention to you, or those who wish to buy it.
Er nú ok ekki vel felld vist þín vilgis lengi hér í Nóregi, því at ek þykkjumst sjá, hvern Haraldr konungr vill þinn hlut, ef hann á at ráða, sem hann mun ráða, ef þú ert lengi í Nóregi".	Then now also I well end hospitality yours very long here in Norway, because that I think so, who Harald the-king will your matter, if he has the decision, as he shall decide, if you are long in Norway".	Then I will also end your very long stay here in Norway, because I think that King Harald will do to you, if he gets the chance, and he shall do what he wants if you stay here much longer".
Nú gaf Magnús konungr honum silfr fyrir hólminn ok vill nú eigi þar hætta honum, ok fór Hreiðarr út til Íslands ok bjó norðr í Svarfaðardal, [þar sem síðan heitir á Hreiðarsstöðum], ok gerist mikill maðr fyrir sér.	Now gave Magnus the-king him silver for the-island and wished now not there endanger him, and travelled Hreidar out to Iceland and settled north in Svarfardal, [there which afterwards is-named by Hreidar's-Place], and became a-great man before himself.	Now King Magnus gave him silver for the island and wished that he now not endanger himself, and Hreidar travelled to Iceland and settled north in Svarfardal, which was afterwards named Hreidar's Place, and he became a great man before himself.

The Tale of Hreiðarr the Fool (Old Norse)

Old Norse	Literal	English
Ok ferr hans ráð mjök eftir getu Magnúss konungs, at þess betr er er meir líðr fram hans ævi, ok hefir hann gert sér at mestum hluta þau kynjalæti, er hann sló á sik inn fyrra hlut ævinnar.	And went his advised much after could Magnus the-king, that this better was that more passed from his life, and had he done himself the most share then eccentricities, that he struck to himself the last-years share of-life.	And his life went much as King Magnus had advised, that his life would get better the more it passed, for he had made up for the greater share of eccentricities that he inflicted on himself in the first part of his life.
Bjó hann til elli í Svarfaðardal, ok eru margir menn frá honum komnir.	Lived he to old-age in Svarfardal, and are many people from him coming.	He lived to old age in Svarfardale and many people are descended from him.
Ok lýkr hér þessi ræðu.	And concluded here this speech.	And here this speech is concluded.

Word List (Old Norse to English)

Old Norse	English

A, a

aðra	other
aðrir	others
af	of, of, off
afbragð	stood-out
afglapa	fool
afl	strength
afli	strength
aflit	strength
afskipti	dealings
aftr	back, before
aldri	age, never, never
aldrigi	never
alla	all
allan	all
alláræðislítill	very-timid
allgóð	all-good
allir	all
allnær	all-near
allr	all
allra	all
allrífligt	all-abundant
alls	all
allstarsýnn	fixed-upon
allt	all, altogether
allundarligt	all-wonderful
allvel	all-well, all-well
alþýðu	all-the-people, the-people
annarr	another
annarra	other
annars	another's, any-other
annast	take-care-of
annat	other, other
at	a, as, at, been, in, is, of, of, on, than, that, that, the, the, to, to, with, with
auga	eye

Á, á

á	about, at, by, for, from, has, in, of, on, so, that, then, to
áðan	earlier
áðr	after, before, returned
ágang	aggression
áheyrsli	to-hear
álpun	rough
átt	had, have, that
átti	had

Æ, æ

ætla	intended, suppose
ætlaði	intended
ætlan	suppose
ætlar	intended, suppose
ævi	life
ævinnar	of-life

B, b

báðir	both
bæði	both
bænum	dwelling, residence
bærist	bearing
banans	death
banni	banned
barðr	beat
batna	better
beiddist	asked
beiðir	asked
beiðzt	asked, best
ber	bear
beri	bear
berr	carry, carrying
betr	better
betra	better
bezt	best

Word List (Old Norse to English)

Old Norse	English
biðja	ask, to-ask
bitbeini	bite-bone
bjó	lived, prepared, settled
Björgyn	Bergen
blásit	trumpet-blast
blíðlíga	joyfully
borðit	table
borit	bear
bóta	compensation
bræðr	brothers
bræðrum	brothers
brátt	soon
breyttu	varied
brjóta	break
bróðir	brother
bróður	a-brother, brother
brögðóttr	tricky
brott	away
brottu	away, steep
brýzt	hammering
bú	prepare
búa	dress
búinn	dressed, prepared
búit	settled
búning	clothing
búnir	offer, prepared
byrgðr	closed

D, d

Old Norse	English
dæmð	to-deem
dála	bad
dauðr	dead
dofna	numb
draga	draw
dregst	drawn
drepa	kill, to-kill
drepi	kill
drepið	kill
drepinn	killed
drykkju	drinking
dylja	disguise

E, e

Old Norse	English
eða	and, but, either, or
ef	if, of
efnin	materials
eftir	after, afterwards
eiga	had, have, own
eigi	none, not, nothing, one-thing
eigu	have
einhverju	once
einkum	especially
einn	alone, one
einrænligu	eccentric
eins	one's
einu	a
einum	alone, one
eirir	own
eitt	once, one
eitthvert	one
ek	i, is
ekki	i, is-not, not
elli	old-age
elligar	otherwise
em	am
en	and, but, than, that, the, then, when
enda	and
engar	no
engi	no, none, no-one
engri	no
engu	none
enn	but, that, then
er	am, am-i, are, as, be, being, but, has, i, in, is, that, the, then, to, to-be, was, were, what, when, where, which, who, whom, would
era	are
erendi	business
erendit	errand
ert	are
ertu	are-you

Word List (Old Norse to English)

Old Norse	English
eru	are, they-are, was, were
eruð	are
Eyjafirði	Eyjafjord
Eyvindar	Eyvind
Eyvindr	Eyvind

F, f

Old Norse	English
fá	get, give
fæ	give
fæðist	born
fær	can
færa	bring
færði	brought
færðr	brought
færi	bring
færr	capable
fágar	cleaned
fagna	welcomed
fáir	few
fallin	fallen
fallit	fallen
fann	found
fara	go, going, to-be, to-go, travel, travelled, went
farar	journey
fari	travel, travelled
farið	go
farit	fared, going
fastr	secure
fátt	few, little
fauk	drifted
fé	fee, money
feld	cloak
feldinum	cloak
felld	end, shed
felldr	situated
fellr	fell
fellt	falling
fenginn	given
fer	go
ferð	travel, travelled
ferðina	travelling

Old Norse	English
ferligu	monstrous
ferr	goes, passed, travelled, went
finn	find
finna	find, found
finnast	meet, meet-up, met
finnst	found
finnumst	find
firna	criticised
fjandligr	fiendish
fjárins	of-wealth
fjárskakka	uneven-share
fjölmenni	followers, followers-many
fjölmennit	many-people
fjölmennt	crowded
flesta	most
fleygir	threw
flokk	group
fluttir	brought
flytr	transport
föðurarf	inheritance
fór	travelled, went
för	going, travelled, travelling
förin	for-travelling, travelling
förna	sacrificing
forræði	self-control
förum	go, going, trading-voyages, travelling
föruneyti	companionship
föruneytis	company
forvitni	curious
fót	foot
frá	away-from, from
frændi	kinsman, kinsmen
fráleik	from-game
fráleikrinn	game, swiftness
fram	from
frammi	from
frávastr	swift
fréttir	news
fríðenda	good-things
fund	find, meet, visit
fundar	to-meet

Word List (Old Norse to English)

Old Norse	English
fundarins	the-meeting
fundit	found
fundu	found
fúsastr	wished
fylgið	follow
fylgjusamr	follow-same
fylgt	follow
fyrir	ahead, along, before, for, from, in-front-of
fyrirgert	fore-done
fyrr	before
fyrra	last-years
fyrst	first
fyrstu	first

G, g

Old Norse	English
gæfu	be-gifted
gæti	got
gætt	taken-care-of
gaf	gave
gafst	gave
gaman	fun, game
gamni	amuse
ganga	go, going, went
gat	got
gátu	got
gefa	gave, give, to-give
gefr	give
gefst	gave
gekk	went
geng	go
gengr	go, going, walked, went
gera	did, do, done
geri	do
gerik	do
gerir	did, made
gerist	became
gerla	completely
gerr	made
gert	did, done, made
gerzt	done, made
get	guess, mention
getit	told
getr	get
getu	could
geysihagliga	exceedingly-skilful
ginna	mocking
ginningar	mocking
glíkligt	favourable
glíkr	like
Glúmr	Glum
góða	good
góðan	good
góðum	good
góma	gums
gott	god, good
gramir	anger
grán	grey
grandi	injury
greipr	grasp
greitt	ready-to-serve
gripr	treasure
gropasamliga	grouped-together
grösum	grass
gull	gold
gyllt	gold
gyltr	young-sow

H, h

Old Norse	English
háðs	mockery
háðungar	insult
hæð	height
hægra	easy
hætta	conclude, endanger
hætti	way
haf	sea
hafa	had, have
hafði	had
hafi	have
hafir	have
hagr	benefit, handy, skilled
halda	held, rather
haldi	hold
haldist	rather
hálft	half
hálfu	half
handkrækjumst	hands-hook-us

Word List (Old Norse to English)

Old Norse	English	*Old Norse*	English
hann	he, him, it	*hirðmaðr*	court-man
hans	he, him, his	*hirðmann*	court-man
Harald	Harald	*hirðmönnum*	court-men
Haraldi	Harald	*hirðvistar*	court, court-visit
Haraldr	Harald, Harald's	*hitt*	find, it, this
Haralds	Harald's	*hitta*	meet
harðleikit	hardness	*hittast*	met
hart	hard	*hitti*	met
háttung	risk	*hittir*	found
hefði	having	*hjá*	beside, by
hefi	have	*hlægi*	ridicule
hefir	had, has, have	*hlæjandi*	laughing
hefnt	revenge	*hlær*	laughed
heftir	have	*hleypr*	ran
heilinn	brain	*hljóp*	ran
heill	a-complete, the-whole, whole	*hljóta*	luck
heim	home	*hló*	laughed
heima	at-home	*hlotit*	bound-to
heimil	home	*hlut*	matter, share
heitir	is-named	*hluta*	share
heldr	behold, rather	*hlutar*	share
heljar	death	*hlutr*	share
helzt	rather	*hlýða*	listened
hendi	hand	*hlýddið*	listen-to
hendr	hand	*hóf*	in-moderation
hendu	handed	*höfði*	head
hentr	suited	*höfðinu*	head
hér	here	*höfðu*	had
herbergi	room	*hófi*	measure
herra	lord	*höfum*	have
hest	horse	*hógværr*	humble
hesta	horse	*hólminn*	the-island
hestinn	the-horse	*hólmr*	small-island
hestr	a-horse	*hon*	it
hestrinn	horse's	*hönd*	hand
hestum	horses	*höndin*	hand
hét	promised, was-named	*höndum*	handed, seized
heyra	heard	*honum*	he, him, it
heyrðak	heard	*horn*	corners
heyrði	heard	*hornblástr*	trumpet-blast
heyrir	heard	*hræddr*	worried
heyrt	heard	*Hreiðar*	Hreidar
hinnig	there	*Hreiðari*	Hreidar
hirðarinnar	court	*Hreiðarr*	Hreidar
hirðinni	court, court-men	*Hreiðars*	Hreidar

Word List (Old Norse to English)

Old Norse	English
Hreiðarssonar	Son-of-Hreidar
Hreiðarsstöðum	Hreidar's-Place
hríð	awhile
hring	a-ring
hrundu	teased
hrutu	fell
hug	thought
hugði	thought
hugkvæmir	very-smart
hugkvæmr	ingenuity
hugr	think
hurðina	the-door
húsi	house
hvar	where
hvárt	how, whether
hvat	how, what
hvé	how
hvergi	nowhere
hverju	what
hverjum	each, everyone
hvern	each, who
hvernig	how, which
hverr	each, every, what
hversu	how-so
hví	why
hvíldar	rest
hygg	minded
hyggðu	think
hyggr	considered, looked, think

I, i

illa	badly
illt	bad, badly, ill
inn	in, the
innast	do
it	that, the, to

Í, í

í	as, at, by, from, in, of, so, the, to, with
ísinn	his
Ísland	Iceland
Íslands	Iceland
íslendingar	icelander

J, j

já	yes
jafnan	always, equally
jafnmæli	equal-speak
jafnt	equally
jafnvel	equally-well

K, k

kæja	disturbed
kæmi	came
kæmir	come
kæmist	come
kallaðr	called
kallar	called
kann	can, know
kaupa	buy
kemr	came
kenna	knew
kjósa	choose
klæðum	clothes
kné	knees
kom	came, come
koma	came, come, coming, to-come
komi	come
kominn	came, come, coming
komit	came, come
komnir	coming
kómu	came
konung	the-king
konunga	kings
konungar	kings, the-kings
konungi	the-king
konunginn	the-king
konungr	king, the-king
konungs	king, the-king, the-king's
korn	came

Word List (Old Norse to English)

Old Norse	English
krummur	hands
kvað	said, spoke
kvæði	poem, the-poem
kvæðislaunin	poem-reward
kvæðit	poem, the-poem
kveðju	greeting
kveðr	greeted, recited, spoke
kykvendum	some-beast
kynjalæti	eccentricities
kynlig	strange
kynligast	strangely
kynligu	strange

L, l

Old Norse	English
læti	noise
lætr	had, leaves
lagði	had
lagðr	had, laid
lagi	lead
land	land
landi	the-land
langar	long
langt	long
lát	have
láta	allow, be, be-allowed, have, left
latliga	negligently
lattan	dissuade
látum	have
launungu	secretly
laust	let-go
leggja	allow, let, take
leggr	have, laid
leið	way
leiðast	carried-out, hand
leik	sport
leikmikill	playful
leikrinn	the-game
leit	looked
leitat	sought
lék	played
lends	land
lengi	long
lét	had
létu	had
leyfa	allow
leyfi	leave
leyfir	leave
leyft	given-leave
leysa	redeem
lézt	let
liði	company
líðr	passed, passes
liðs	company
liðu	passed
líkar	like, liked
líkast	like
líkr	like
líta	company
lítill	a-little, small
lítils	little
lítit	little
litlu	a-little
litu	noticed
lízt	appears
ljótari	uglier
ljótr	ugly
ljúga	lie
lofgjarnliga	praise-will
loft	lift
lögðu	had
lokit	ended
lokka	lure
lundhægr	even-spirit, tempered-even
lýkr	concluded

M, m

Old Norse	English
má	may
maðr	a-man, man, people
maðrinn	a-man
mæl	say
mæla	discuss
mælgina	talking
mælik	speak
mælir	spoke
mælt	speaking, spoken

Word List (Old Norse to English)

Old Norse	English
mælti	said, spoke
mæltir	speak
mæltu	spoke
mætti	may
Magnús	Magnus
Magnúsi	Magnus
Magnúss	Magnus, Magnus's
mál	matter, matters, way
máli	speak
málinu	the-matter
málit	discuss
málugr	talkative
mann	man, that-man
manna	a-man, men, people, the-men
mannfátt	people-few
manni	of-the-people
manninn	the-man
manninum	the-people
mannraunum	human-trials
manns	man
marga	many
margir	many
margs	many
margt	many
mark	sign
mátti	it-may
máttu	may, may-you
mazt	most
með	among, as, with
mega	may
meiddr	hurt
meir	further, more
meira	more
menn	men, people
mennskr	human
mér	i, me, mine, my, to-me
mest	most
mesta	most
mestum	most
miðlungi	poorly
mik	i, me, much
mikil	much
mikill	a-great, great, tall
mikinn	great

Old Norse	English
mikit	large, many, much
miklum	much
milli	between
mín	me, mine
mína	mine
mínar	mine
minn	mine
minna	less
minni	less
míns	mine
mitt	me, mine, my
mjök	much
mönnum	men, people
morgin	morning
morgininn	morning
mörgu	many-ways
mörgum	many
mót	against
móti	meeting, of
mótinu	meeting
mótit	meeting, meetings
móts	meet, meetings
mun	could, may, must, shall, should, would
muna	should
mund	time
mundi	would
muni	would
munni	mouth
munt	shall-you
muntu	shall-you, should-you
munu	shall
myndi	should, would
myndir	would

N, n

Old Norse	English
naddar	studded
nær	near
nálægir	near-lying
námu	took
nauðsyn	need
nema	except
nemr	took
nestlokum	the-end

Word List (Old Norse to English)

Old Norse	English
niðr	down
njót	enjoy
nökkur	somewhat
nökkura	some
nökkurri	some
nökkut	of-any, some, something
norðr	north
Nóreg	Norway
Nóregi	Norway
nú	now
nýkominn	newly-come
nýt	used
nytjar	use

O, o

Old Norse	English
ofar	above
ofsögum	off-said
oft	frequently
ok	also, and
okkarn	ours
okkart	ours
okkr	ours, us, you
orð	words
orðit	words
orðsending	message
orðum	words
orðvarr	discreet
ort	worded
oss	us

Ó, ó

Old Norse	English
óbúinn	unprepared
ófælinn	without-fear
ógreið	un-passable
óheilagr	unholy
óknáleik	prowess
ólatr	not-forget
ólið	unaccompanied
ólíkast	unlike
ólíkligt	unlikely
ómállatr	chatty, talkative
ónýtt	ruined
ór	out-of
ósannligt	untrue
ósýknligr	un-innocent-looking
óvanr	un-accustomed
óvart	un-warned
óvísu	unknown

Ö, ö

Old Norse	English
öðru	others
öðrum	other, others
ökulbrókum	ankle-breeches
öllu	all
öllum	all
öxarsköft	axe-handles

P, p

Old Norse	English
penninga	money

R, r

Old Norse	English
ráð	advice, advised, decide
ráða	advice, advise, decide, decision
ráðligra	advisable
ræða	discuss
ræðu	speech
rammi	frame
réði	decide
reið	rode
reiðar	ride
reiðast	anger
reiðfara	voyage
reiði	anger
reiðin	uproar
reiðina	anger
reiðingum	uproar
reiðist	angered
reiðr	angry
reiðumst	become-angry

Word List (Old Norse to English)

Old Norse	English
reikuð	roughly-handled
rennr	run
reyna	test
reynt	tried
rjáðr	worried

S, s

Old Norse	English
sá	saw, so, such, that
sæja	see
sæki	conviction
sæmiliga	well-enough
sætt	settled, settlement
sættir	settle
sagða	said
sagði	said
sagt	said, told
sakar	conviction, reasons
sama	himself
saman	together
samdægris	same-day
samir	in-common
samtengja	unite
sanna	truth
sannast	true
satt	true
sáttarfundar	peace-meeting
sáttarfundr	peace-meeting
sáttir	agreed
sátu	sat
saurgar	dirty
sé	as, be, being, he, is, see, seeing, seen, so, you
sefr	sleeps
seg	tell
segir	said, say, told
segja	said, say, told
seint	slowly
selja	sell
selr	sell
sem	as, how, like, such, which
senda	send, sending
sendan	sent
sendi	send, sent
senn	they, together
sér	he, him, himself, his, saw, see, so
sét	seen
setr	set
sex	six
síðan	after, afterwards, then
síðar	afterwards
síðr	less
sigla	sailed
sik	him, himself, such, themselves
silfr	silver
silfri	silver
silfrit	silver
sín	theirs
sína	he, his
sinn	his, occasion
sinni	this
sínum	his
sitja	sit, sitting
sitt	his
sjá	saw, see, seemed, seen, so, to-see
sjálfan	myself
sjálfbjargi	self-supported
sjálfir	themselves
sjálfr	himself, self, yourself
skal	shall, should
skálpana	scabbards
skaltu	shall-you
skammt	short-distance
skap	mood
skapi	character
skauttogaðr	roughly
skauttoguðu	pull-cloak, handle-roughly
skeindist	scratched
skerum	cut
skikkju	cloak
skikkjuna	cloak
skilði	parted
skilðir	parted
skilðust	separated
skilja	parted, understand

Word List (Old Norse to English)

Old Norse	English
skilst	separate
skip	ship
skipa	exchange
skipast	changed
skipdráttar	ship-launching
skjótt	swiftly
skógar	woods
skógum	the-woods
skömmu	recently
skortir	shortage
skrúðklæðin	costly-clothing
skulir	should
skulu	shall
skulum	shall, should
skýla	protect
skyldast	obliged
skyldi	should
skyldu	should
skýtr	throws
slíkt	such
sló	struck
smátt	small
smíðaði	making
smíðat	crafted, made, smithery
smíðinni	smith, the-work
snemma	early
sögðu	said
sögu	story
sökum	blame, sake
sönnu	true
sótti	took
spenar	suckling
spotti	small
spurði	asked
spyrr	asked, learned
srterkr	strong
stað	place
staðar	place
staðinn	standing
stæða	stand
standa	stand, standing
standi	stand
stefnt	located
stendr	stood
sterkr	strong

Old Norse	English
stofuna	the-room
stofunni	the-room
stórvirkja	great-work
stukku	leapt
stund	awhile, time
stundir	while
stundu	time
stundum	awhile, sometimes
svá	seen, so
svaraði	answered
svarar	answered
Svarfaðardal	Svarfardal
sverðskónum	sword-studded
svín	a-pig
svíninu	the-pig
svínit	the-pig
sýndi	showed
sýnist	seemed, seems

T, t

Old Norse	English
tak	take
taka	take
tákna	betoken
táknar	taken
tal	talk
tala	talk
talat	told
tek	took
tekr	take, took
tíðenda	news
tíðendi	news
tíðir	wish
tigu	tens
til	to, until
tilgerðir	to-do
tjáir	express
tók	took
töluðu	talked
torsótt	difficulty
trautt	scarcely
treystumst	we-trust
tröll	monstrous
trúi	trust
tvá	two

Word List (Old Norse to English)

Old Norse	English
tvau	two

Þ, þ

Old Norse	English
þá	then
þaðan	from-there
þætti	seemed, seems
þættist	thought
þættumst	we-have
þangat	from-here, there
þann	he, then, then
þannig	thus
þar	then, there, they
þarftu	need-you
þars	there
þat	is, it, that, the, this
þ-at	it
þau	then
þaut	shrill
þegar	already, as-soon, as-soon-as, from-there, soon, straightaway, then, there, when
þegi	silent
þeim	the, them, they
þeir	their, they
þeira	them, they
þenna	that
þér	to-you, you, your
þess	this
þessa	this
þessarar	this-kind-of
þessi	these, this
þessir	these
þessu	this
þessum	this
þetta	that, this
þeygi	yet-not
þik	you
þín	you, yours
þína	your, yours
þingit	assembly
þingsins	their-assembly
þinn	your, yours
þitt	the, your, yours
þó	though
Þórð	Thord
Þórðar	Thord's
Þórðr	Thord
Þorgrímsson	Son-of-Thorgrim
þótt	though, thought
þótti	thought
þóttist	thought
þraut	faltered
þreytti	tired
þrotinn	ended
þú	though, you
þurfa	need, needed
þvarr	decreased
þvegnar	to-wash
því	accordingly, because, before, for, otherwise, since, such, then, therefore, this
þvílíkt	therefore-like
þykkir	felt, seemed, think, thought
þykkist	seems, think, thought
þykkja	to-think
þykkjast	consider
þykkjumst	think

U, u

Old Norse	English
um	about, around
umbóta	put-right
umsjá	about, guidance
undan	away, away-from
undarliga	strange
undarligr	a-strange
undarligt	wonderful
undir	under
unga	young
unnit	done
unz	until
upp	up
upplönd	uplands
uppstert	upright

Word List (Old Norse to English)

Old Norse	English
Ú, ú	
út	away, out
útan	out
úti	out
V, v	
vá	killed
vaðmál	homespun-cloth
vaðmálsklæði	wadding-clothes
vælir	wilful
vænleikr	handsome
vænn	handsome
vænsta	good
væri	was, were, will-be
væria	be
værir	be
vaki	wake
vaknaðir	woken
valdit	wielded
vanbúinn	unprepared
vandamál	disputes
vandara	important
vandliga	closely
vandligar	carefully
vánir	custom
vant	difficult
vápnum	weapons
var	was, were
varla	hardly, scarcely
várn	ours
varr	aware
várr	ours
váru	were
vaskligr	valiant
vega	ways
veggr	a-wall
vegit	slain
vegr	proceeded
veit	knew, know, knows
veitt	given
veittir	grant
veizlu	feast
veiztu	know-you
vel	well
velja	will
ver	be
vér	we
vera	be, become, being
verð	worth
verða	be, became, become, was
verði	became, become, becomes, was
verðr	became, become, becomes, were
verit	been
verr	worse
verri	worse
verst	worse
vetri	winter
vetrvistar	winter-provisions
vexti	grown
við	against, as, from, of, to, with
víðförull	widely-travelled
víginu	the-slaying
vil	will, wish
vilda	willed, wish, wished
vildi	willed, wished
vildir	would
vildu	wiled
vilgis	very
vilja	wish-to
vill	well, will, wish, wished, wishes, would
villt	wish
villtu	will-you, wish-you
vináttu	friendship
vindli	wind
vinveitt	friendly
virðir	worth
vist	hospitality
víst	certainly
vistin	stay
vísu	certainly
vit	know, we
vita	know, knowing

Word List (Old Norse to English)

Old Norse	English
viti	knowing
vitrari	wiser
vitrligra	wisely
vits	wits
vizkumaðr	wise-man

Y, y

yðr	you, your
yðvarn	you
yðvars	yours
yfir	about, over
ykkar	you
ykkr	you

Ý, ý

ýmsu	variously

Word List *(English to Old Norse)*

English	Old Norse
A, a	
about	á, á, á, á
at	á, á, á
after	áðr, áðr, ætla
aggression	ágang
age	aldri
all	alla, allan, allgóð, allir, allnær, allr, allra, allrífligt, alls
all-good	allgóð
all-near	allnær
all-abundant	allrífligt
altogether	allt
all-wonderful	allundarligt
all-well	allvel, allvel
all-the-people	alþýðu
another	annarr
another's	annars
any-other	annars
a	at, at
as	at, at, at, at, at, átt, átt
asked	beiddist, beiðir, beiðzt, beiðzt, ber
ask	biðja
a-brother	bróður
away	brott, brottu, brýzt, búa
and	eða, eða, eða, ef
afterwards	eftir, eiga, eiga
alone	einn, einrænligu
am	em, en
am-i	er
are	er, er, er, er, er
are-you	ertu
away-from	frá, frá
ahead	fyrir
along	fyrir
amuse	gamni
anger	gramir, grán, grandi, greipr
a-complete	heill
at-home	heima
a-horse	hestr
awhile	hríð, hring, hrutu
a-ring	hring
always	jafnan
allow	láta, láta, láta
a-little	lítill, lítils
appears	lízt
a-man	maðr, maðr, maðrinn
among	með
a-great	mikill
against	mót, móti
above	ofar
also	ok
ankle-breeches	ökulbrókum
axe-handles	öxarsköft
advice	ráð, ráð
advised	ráð
advise	ráða
advisable	ráðligra
angered	reiðist
angry	reiðr
agreed	sáttir
answered	svaraði, svarar
a-pig	svín
already	þegar
as-soon	þegar
as-soon-as	þegar
assembly	þingit
accordingly	því
around	um
a-strange	undarligr
aware	varr
a-wall	veggr
B, b	
by	á, á, á
before	áðr, ætla, ætlaði, ætlar, ævi
back	aftr
been	at, at
both	báðir, bæði

Word List (English to Old Norse)

English	Old Norse	English	Old Norse
bearing	*bærist*	closed	*byrgðr*
banned	*banni*	can	*fær, færa*
beat	*barðr*	capable	*færr*
better	*batna, beiddist, beiðir*	cleaned	*fágar*
best	*beiðzt, ber*	cloak	*feld, feldinum, felld, fellr*
bear	*ber, beri, berr*		
bite-bone	*bitbeini*	criticised	*firna*
Bergen	*Björgyn*	crowded	*fjölmennt*
brothers	*bræðr, bræðrum*	companionship	*föruneyti*
break	*brjóta*	company	*föruneytis, forvitni, fót, frá*
brother	*bróðir, bróður*		
bad	*dála, dauðr*	curious	*forvitni*
but	*eða, eða, ef, efnin*	completely	*gerla*
be	*er, er, er, er, er, er, er, era*	could	*getu, geysihagliga*
		conclude	*hætta*
being	*er, er, er*	court	*hirðarinnar, hirðinni, hirðinni*
business	*erendi*		
born	*fæðist*	court-men	*hirðinni, hirðmaðr*
bring	*færa, færði*	court-man	*hirðmaðr, hirðmann*
brought	*færði, færðr, færi*	court-visit	*hirðvistar*
be-gifted	*gæfu*	corners	*horn*
became	*gerist, gerla, gerr, gert*	considered	*hyggr*
benefit	*hagr*	came	*kæmi, kæmir, kæmist, kallaðr, kallar, kann, kann, kaupa*
brain	*heilinn*		
behold	*heldr*		
beside	*hjá*	come	*kæmir, kæmist, kallaðr, kallar, kann, kann, kaupa*
bound-to	*hlotit*		
badly	*illa, illt*	called	*kallaðr, kallar*
buy	*kaupa*	choose	*kjósa*
be-allowed	*láta*	clothes	*klæðum*
between	*milli*	coming	*koma, komi, kominn*
become-angry	*reiðumst*	carried-out	*leiðast*
blame	*sökum*	concluded	*lýkr*
betoken	*tákna*	chatty	*ómállatr*
because	*því*	conviction	*sæki, sakar*
become	*vera, vera, verða, verða*	character	*skapi*
		cut	*skerum*
becomes	*verði, verðr*	changed	*skipast*
		costly-clothing	*skrúðklæðin*

C, c

		crafted	*smíðat*
		consider	*þykkjast*
carry	*berr*	closely	*vandliga*
carrying	*berr*	carefully	*vandligar*
compensation	*bóta*	custom	*vánir*
clothing	*búning*	certainly	*víst, vísu*

Word List (English to Old Norse)

English	*Old Norse*	English	*Old Norse*
		each	*hverjum, hverjum, hvern*
		everyone	*hverjum*

D, d

English	*Old Norse*
dealings	*afskipti*
dwelling	*bænum*
death	*banans, banni*
dress	*búa*
dressed	*búinn*
dead	*dauðr*
draw	*draga*
drawn	*dregst*
drinking	*drykkju*
disguise	*dylja*
drifted	*fauk*
did	*gera, gera, gera*
do	*gera, gera, geri, gerik*
done	*gera, geri, gerik, gerir*
disturbed	*kæja*
dissuade	*lattan*
discuss	*mæla, mætti, Magnús*
down	*niðr*
discreet	*orðvarr*
decide	*ráð, ráða, ráða*
decision	*ráða*
dirty	*saurgar*
decreased	*þvarr*
difficulty	*torsótt*
disputes	*vandamál*
difficult	*vant*

E, e

earlier	*áðan*
eye	*auga*
either	*eða*
especially	*einkum*
eccentric	*einrænligu*
errand	*erendit*
Eyjafjord	*Eyjafirði*
Eyvind	*Eyvindar, Eyvindr*
end	*felld*
exceedingly-skilful	*geysihagliga*
easy	*hægra*
endanger	*hætta*

every	*hverr*
equally	*jafnan, jafnmæli*
equal-speak	*jafnmæli*
equally-well	*jafnvel*
eccentricities	*kynjalæti*
ended	*lokit, lokka*
even-spirit	*lundhægr*
except	*nema*
enjoy	*njót*
exchange	*skipa*
early	*snemma*
express	*tjáir*

F, f

for	*á, á, á*
from	*á, á, á, áðan, áðr, áðr, ætla*
fool	*afglapa*
fixed-upon	*allstarsýnn*
few	*fáir, fallin*
fallen	*fallin, fallit*
found	*fann, fara, fara, farar, farið, farit*
fared	*farit*
fee	*fé*
fell	*fellr, fellt*
falling	*fellt*
find	*finn, finna, finna, finnast, finnast*
fiendish	*fjandligr*
followers	*fjölmenni*
followers-many	*fjölmenni*
for-travelling	*förin*
foot	*fót*
from-game	*fráleik*
follow	*fylgið, fylgjusamr*
follow-same	*fylgjusamr*
fore-done	*fyrirgert*
first	*fyrst, fyrstu*
fun	*gaman*
favourable	*glíkligt*

51

Word List (English to Old Norse)

English	*Old Norse*	English	*Old Norse*
further	*meir*	grown	*vexti*
frequently	*oft*		
frame	*rammi*		
from-there	*þaðan, þangat*		
from-here	*þangat*		
faltered	*braut*		
felt	*þykkir*		
feast	*veizlu*		
friendship	*vináttu*		
friendly	*vinveitt*		

H, h

English	*Old Norse*
has	*á, á, áðan*
had	*átt, átt, átti, auga, báðir, bæði, bænum, bærist, banans, banni, barðr, batna, beiddist*
have	*átt, átti, auga, báðir, bæði, bænum, bærist, banans, banni, barðr, batna, beiddist, beiðir, beiðzt*
hammering	*brýzt*
height	*hæð*
handy	*hagr*
held	*halda*
hold	*haldi*
half	*hálft, hálfu*
hands-hook-us	*handkrækjumst*
he	*hann, hann, hann, hans, hans, hans, Harald*
him	*hann, hann, hans, hans, hans*
his	*hans, Harald, Haraldi, Haraldr, Haraldr, Haralds, harðleikit*
Harald	*Harald, Haraldi, Haraldr*
Harald's	*Haraldr, Haralds*
hardness	*harðleikit*
hard	*hart*
having	*hefði*
home	*heim, heima*
hand	*hendi, hendr, hendu, hér, herra*
handed	*hendu, hér*
here	*hér*
horse	*hest, hesta*
horse's	*hestrinn*
horses	*hestum*
heard	*heyra, heyrðak, heyrði, heyrir, heyrt*
head	*höfði, höfðinu*

G, g

English	*Old Norse*
get	*fá, fá*
give	*fá, fæ, fæðist, fær*
go	*fara, fara, farar, farið, farit, farit, fátt*
going	*fara, farar, farið, farit, farit, fátt*
given	*fenginn, fer*
goes	*ferr*
group	*flokk*
game	*fráleikrinn, fram*
good-things	*fríðenda*
got	*gæti, gaf, gafst*
gave	*gaf, gafst, gaman, gaman*
guess	*get*
Glum	*Glúmr*
good	*góða, góðan, góðum, góma, gott*
gums	*góma*
god	*gott*
grey	*grán*
grasp	*greipr*
grouped-together	*gropasamliga*
grass	*grösum*
gold	*gull, gyllt*
greeting	*kveðju*
greeted	*kveðr*
given-leave	*leyft*
great	*mikill, mikinn*
great-work	*stórvirkja*
guidance	*umsjá*
grant	*veittir*

Word List (English to Old Norse)

English	*Old Norse*	English	*Old Norse*
humble	*hógværr*	**J, j**	
Hreidar	*Hreiðar, Hreiðari, Hreiðarr, Hreiðars*		
Hreidar's-Place	*Hreiðarsstöðum*	joyfully	*blíðlíga*
house	*húsi*	journey	*farar*
how	*hvárt, hvat, hvé, hverjum, hverjum*	**K, k**	
how-so	*hversu*		
hands	*krummur*		
human-trials	*mannraunum*	kill	*drepa, drepi, drepið*
hurt	*meiddr*	killed	*drepinn, drykkju*
human	*mennskr*	kinsman	*frændi*
himself	*sama, samir, sáttir, saurgar*	kinsmen	*frændi*
		know	*kann, kaupa, kemr, kenna*
homespun-cloth	*vaðmál*	knew	*kenna, kjósa*
handsome	*vænleikr, vænn*	knees	*kné*
hardly	*varla*	kings	*konunga, konungar*
hospitality	*vist*	king	*konungr, konungs*
		knows	*veit*
I, i		know-you	*veiztu*
		knowing	*vita, viti*
in	*á, áðan, áðr, áðr, ætla*		
intended	*ætla, ætlaði, ætlar*	**L, l**	
is	*at, átt, átt, átti, auga*		
if	*ef*	life	*ævi*
i	*ek, ek, ekki, ekki, em*	lived	*bjó*
is-not	*ekki*	little	*fátt, fauk, fé*
inheritance	*föðurarf*	last-years	*fyrra*
in-front-of	*fyrir*	like	*glíkr, Glúmr, góða, góðan, góðum*
injury	*grandi*		
insult	*háðungar*	lord	*herra*
it	*hann, hans, hans, hans, Harald, Haraldi*	laughing	*hlæjandi*
		laughed	*hlær, hljóta*
is-named	*heitir*	luck	*hljóta*
in-moderation	*hóf*	listened	*hlýða*
ingenuity	*hugkvæmr*	listen-to	*hlýddið*
ill	*illt*	looked	*hyggr, í*
Iceland	*Ísland, Íslands*	leaves	*lætr*
icelander	*íslendingar*	laid	*lagðr, lagi*
it-may	*mátti*	lead	*lagi*
in-common	*samir*	land	*land, langar*
important	*vandara*	long	*langar, langt, lát*
		left	*láta*
		let-go	*laust*

Word List (English to Old Norse)

English	*Old Norse*	English	*Old Norse*
let	*leggja, leggr*	me	*mér, mér, mér, mest*
leave	*leyfi, leyfir*	mine	*mér, mér, mest, mesta, mestum, mik, mik*
liked	*líkar*		
lie	*ljúga*		
lift	*loft*	my	*mér, mest*
lure	*lokka*	much	*mik, mikil, mikill, mikill, mikinn*
large	*mikit*		
less	*minna, minni, míns*	morning	*morgin, morgininn*
learned	*spyrr*	many-ways	*mörgu*
located	*stefnt*	meeting	*móti, mótinu, mótit*
leapt	*stukku*	meetings	*mótit, móts*
		must	*mun*
		mouth	*munni*
		message	*orðsending*
		myself	*sjálfan*
		mood	*skap*
		making	*smíðaði*

M, m

N, n

English	*Old Norse*
materials	*efnin*
money	*fé, feld*
monstrous	*ferligu, ferr*
meet	*finnast, finnast, finnast, finnst*
meet-up	*finnast*
met	*finnast, finnst, finnumst*
many-people	*fjölmennit*
most	*flesta, flokk, fluttir, föðurarf, för*
made	*gerir, gerist, gerla, gerr, gert*
mention	*get*
mocking	*ginna, ginningar*
mockery	*háðs*
matter	*hlut, hlýða*
measure	*hófi*
minded	*hygg*
may	*má, maðr, maðr, maðrinn, mæla*
man	*maðr, maðrinn, mæla*
Magnus	*Magnús, Magnúsi, Magnúss*
Magnus's	*Magnúss*
matters	*mál*
men	*manna, mannraunum, manns*
many	*marga, margir, margs, margt, mátti, máttu*
may-you	*máttu*
more	*meir, meira*

English	*Old Norse*
never	*aldri, aldri, aldrigi*
numb	*dofna*
none	*eigi, eigi, eigi*
not	*eigi, eigi*
nothing	*eigi*
no	*engar, engi, engi*
no-one	*engi*
news	*fréttir, fund, fundar*
nowhere	*hvergi*
noise	*læti*
negligently	*latliga*
noticed	*litu*
near	*nær*
near-lying	*nálægir*
need	*nauðsyn, nemr*
north	*norðr*
Norway	*Nóreg, Nóregi*
now	*nú*
newly-come	*nýkominn*
not-forget	*ólatr*
need-you	*þarftu*
needed	*þurfa*

Word List (English to Old Norse)

English	Old Norse

O, o

English	Old Norse
of	á, á, á, á, á, á, áðr, aðra, aðrir
on	á, á
other	aðra, aðrir, ætla, ætlan, ætlar
others	aðrir, ætla, ætlan
of-life	ævinnar
off	af
offer	búnir
or	eða
own	eiga, eigi
one-thing	eigi
once	einhverju, einn
one	einn, eins, einum, eirir
one's	eins
old-age	elli
otherwise	elligar, en
of-wealth	fjárins
of-the-people	manni
of-any	nökkut
off-said	ofsögum
ours	okkarn, okkart, okkr, okkr, okkr
out-of	ór
occasion	sinn
obliged	skyldast
out	út, útan, úti
over	yfir

P, p

English	Old Norse
prepared	bjó, bjó, blásit
prepare	bú
passed	ferr, ferr, ferr
promised	hét
poem	kvæði, kvæði
poem-reward	kvæðislaunin
playful	leikmikill
played	lék
passes	líðr
praise-will	lofgjarnliga
people	maðr, mæl, mælgina, mælik
people-few	mannfátt
poorly	miðlungi
prowess	óknáleik
peace-meeting	sáttarfundar, sáttarfundr
pull-cloak, handle-roughly	skauttoguðu
parted	skilði, skilðir, skilðust
protect	skýla
place	stað, staðar
put-right	umbóta
proceeded	vegr

R, r

English	Old Norse
returned	áðr
rough	álpun
residence	bænum
ready-to-serve	greitt
rather	halda, haldist, háttung, hefnt
risk	háttung
revenge	hefnt
room	herbergi
ridicule	hlægi
ran	hleypr, hljóp
rest	hvíldar
recited	kveðr
redeem	leysa
ruined	ónýtt
rode	reið
ride	reiðar
roughly-handled	reikuð
run	rennr
reasons	sakar
roughly	skauttogaðr
recently	skömmu

S, s

English	Old Norse
so	á, á, á, á, áðr, aðra, aðrir
suppose	ætla, ætlan, ætlar
stood-out	afbragð
strength	afl, afli, aflit

Word List (English to Old Norse)

English	*Old Norse*	English	*Old Norse*
settled	*bjó, blásit, borðit*	something	*nökkut*
soon	*brátt, breyttu*	speech	*ræðu*
steep	*brottu*	saw	*sá, sá, sá*
secure	*fastr*	such	*sá, sá, sæja, sæmiliga, sætt*
shed	*felld*		
situated	*felldr*	see	*sæja, sæmiliga, sætt, sætt*
sacrificing	*förna*		
self-control	*forræði*	settlement	*sætt*
swiftness	*fráleikrinn*	settle	*sættir*
swift	*frávastr*	same-day	*samdægris*
sea	*haf*	sat	*sátu*
skilled	*hagr*	seeing	*sé*
suited	*hentr*	seen	*sé, sé, sé, sefr*
share	*hlut, hluta, hlutar, hlutr*	sleeps	*sefr*
		slowly	*seint*
small-island	*hólmr*	sell	*selja, selr*
seized	*höndum*	send	*senda, senda*
Son-of-Hreidar	*Hreiðarssonar*	sending	*senda*
said	*kvað, kvað, kvæði, kvæði, kvæðislaunin, kvæðit, kvæðit, kveðr*	sent	*sendan, sendi*
		set	*setr*
		six	*sex*
spoke	*kvað, kvæði, kvæði, kvæðislaunin, kvæðit*	sailed	*sigla*
		silver	*silfr, silfri, silfrit*
some-beast	*kykvendum*	sit	*sitja*
strange	*kynlig, kynligast, kynligu*	sitting	*sitja*
		seemed	*sjá, sjá, sjá, sjá*
strangely	*kynligast*	self-supported	*sjálfbjargi*
secretly	*launungu*	self	*sjálfr*
sport	*leik*	scabbards	*skálpana*
sought	*leitat*	short-distance	*skammt*
small	*lítill, litu, ljótari*	scratched	*skeindist*
say	*mæl, mælgina, mælik*	separated	*skilðust*
speak	*mælik, mælir, mælt*	separate	*skilst*
speaking	*mælt*	ship	*skip*
spoken	*mælt*	ship-launching	*skipdráttar*
sign	*mark*	swiftly	*skjótt*
shall	*mun, mun, mun, muna, mund*	shortage	*skortir*
		struck	*sló*
should	*mun, mun, muna, mund, mundi, muni, munt, muntu*	smithery	*smíðat*
		smith	*smíðinni*
		story	*sögu*
shall-you	*munt, muntu, muntu*	sake	*sökum*
should-you	*muntu*	suckling	*spenar*
studded	*naddar*	strong	*srterkr, stað*
somewhat	*nökkur*	standing	*staðinn, stæða*
some	*nökkura, nökkurri, nökkut*		

Word List (English to Old Norse)

English	Old Norse	English	Old Norse
stand	stæða, standa, standa	travelling	ferðina, ferr, ferr, ferr
stood	stendr	threw	fleygir
sometimes	stundum	transport	flytr
Svarfardal	Svarfaðardal	trading-voyages	förum
sword-studded	sverðskónum	to-meet	fundar
showed	sýndi	the-meeting	fundarins
seems	sýnist, tak, taka	taken-care-of	gætt
shrill	þaut	to-give	gefa
straightaway	þegar	told	getit, greitt, gripr, gyltr, hætti
silent	þegi	treasure	gripr
Son-of-Thorgrim	Þorgrímsson	the-whole	heill
since	því	the-horse	hestinn
scarcely	trautt, treystumst	there	hinnig, hitt, hlægi, hleypr, hljóp
slain	vegit	this	hitt, hlægi, hleypr, hljóp, hlut, hluta, hlutar, hlutr, hólminn, hólmr
stay	vistin		

T, t

English	Old Norse	English	Old Norse
that	á, á, á, áðr, aðra, aðrir, ætla, ætlan, ætlar, ævinnar, af, af	the-island	hólminn
		teased	hrundu
then	á, á, áðr, aðra, aðrir, ætla, ætlan, ætlar, ævinnar, af, af, af	thought	hug, hugði, hugkvæmir, hugr, hurðina, hvar, hvárt, hvat
to	á, áðr, aðra, aðrir, ætla, ætlan, ætlar, ævinnar	think	hugr, hurðina, hvar, hvárt, hvat, hvergi
to-hear	áheyrsli	the-door	hurðina
the-people	alþýðu, annarra	to-come	koma
take-care-of	annast	the-king	konung, konungar, konungi, konunginn, konungr
than	at, at		
the	at, at, at, at, at, at, átt, bænum, biðja, bjó	the-kings	konungar
		the-king's	konungs
to-ask	biðja	the-poem	kvæði, kvæðislaunin
trumpet-blast	blásit, borðit	the-land	landi
table	borðit	take	leggja, leið, leik, leikmikill
tricky	brögðóttr		
to-deem	dæmð	the-game	leikrinn
to-kill	drepa	tempered-even	lundhægr
to-be	er, er	talking	mælgina
they-are	eru	the-matter	málinu
to-go	fara	talkative	málugr, mann
travel	fara, fara, fara	that-man	mann
travelled	fara, fara, fari, fari, fastr, felld	the-men	manna
		the-man	manninn
		to-me	mér

Word List (English to Old Norse)

English	Old Norse
tall	mikill
time	mund, mundi, muni
took	námu, nauðsyn, nemr, nestlokum, nökkur, nökkura
the-end	nestlokum
test	reyna
tried	reynt
together	saman, samdægris
truth	sanna
true	sannast, satt, sáttarfundar
tell	seg
they	senn, senn, sér, sér, sér
themselves	sik, silfr
theirs	sín
to-see	sjá
the-woods	skógum
throws	skýtr
the-work	smíðinni
the-room	stofuna, stofunni
the-pig	svíninu, svínit
taken	táknar
talk	tal, tala
thus	þannig
them	þeim, þeim
their	þeir
to-you	þér
this-kind-of	þessarar
these	þessi, þessi
their-assembly	þingsins
though	þó, Þórð, Þórðar
Thord	Þórð, Þórðar
Thord's	Þórðar
tired	þreytti
to-wash	þvegnar
therefore	því
therefore-like	þvílíkt
to-think	þykkja
tens	tigu
to-do	tilgerðir
talked	töluðu
trust	trúi
two	tvá, tvau
the-slaying	víginu

U, u

English	Old Norse
uneven-share	fjárskakka
uglier	ljótari
ugly	ljótr
used	nýt
use	nytjar
unprepared	óbúinn, öðru
un-passable	ógreið
unholy	óheilagr
us	okkr, okkr
unaccompanied	ólið
unlike	ólíkast
unlikely	ólíkligt
untrue	ósannligt
un-innocent-looking	ósýknligr
un-accustomed	óvanr
un-warned	óvart
unknown	óvísu
uproar	reiðin, reiðingum
unite	samtengja
understand	skilja
until	til, tilgerðir
under	undir
up	upp
uplands	upplönd
upright	uppstert

V, v

English	Old Norse
very-timid	alláræðislítill
varied	breyttu
visit	fund
very-smart	hugkvæmir
voyage	reiðfara
valiant	vaskligr
very	vilgis
variously	ýmsu

Word List (English to Old Norse)

English	*Old Norse*	English	*Old Norse*
		well	*vel, velja*
		will	*velja, vér, verð*
		we	*vér, verð*
# W, w		worth	*verð, verða*
with	*at, at, átt, bænum, biðja*	worse	*verr, verri, verst*
when	*en, engar, engi*	winter	*vetri*
was	*er, er, er, er, er, er*	winter-provisions	*vetrvistar*
were	*er, er, er, er, er, er*	widely-travelled	*víðförull*
what	*er, er, er, er*	willed	*vilda, vilda*
where	*er, er*	wiled	*vildu*
which	*er, er, er*	wish-to	*vilja*
who	*er, er*	wishes	*vill*
whom	*er*	will-you	*villtu*
would	*er, eru, eru, eru, fagna, fara, fara, fara*	wish-you	*villtu*
		wind	*vindli*
welcomed	*fagna*	wiser	*vitrari*
went	*fara, fari, fari, fastr, felld, felldr*	wisely	*vitrligra*
		wits	*vits*
wished	*fúsastr, gætt, ganga, gefa*	wise-man	*vizkumaðr*
walked	*gengr*	# Y, y	
way	*hætti, haf, hagr*		
whole	*heill*		
was-named	*hét*	young-sow	*gyltr*
worried	*hræddr, Hreiðarssonar*	yes	*já*
		you	*okkr, óknáleik, ólatr, ólið, ólíkast, ólíkligt, ómállatr, ónýtt, ór, orð*
whether	*hvárt*		
why	*hví*		
without-fear	*ófælinn*		
words	*orð, orðit, orðum*	yourself	*sjálfr*
worded	*ort*	your	*þér, þess, þessa, þessarar, þessi*
well-enough	*sæmiliga*		
woods	*skógar*	yet-not	*þeygi*
while	*stundir*	yours	*þín, þína, þína, þingsins, þinn*
we-have	*þættumst*		
wish	*tíðir, tigu, til, til, tilgerðir*	young	*unga*
we-trust	*treystumst*		
wonderful	*undarligt*		
wadding-clothes	*vaðmálsklæði*		
wilful	*vælir*		
will-be	*væri*		
wake	*vaki*		
woken	*vaknaðir*		
wielded	*valdit*		
weapons	*vápnum*		
ways	*vega*		

The Tale of Hreiðarr the Fool (*Old Icelandic*)

Old Icelandic	Literal	English
1	**1**	**1**
Þórður hét maður.	Thord was-named a-man.	There was a man named Thord.
Hann var Þorgrímsson, Hreiðarssonar, þess er Glúmur vó.	He was Son-of-Thorgrim, Son-of-Hreidar, this whom Glum killed.	He was the son of Thorgrim, the son of Hreidar who killed Glum.
Þórður var lítill maður vexti og vænn.	Thord was a-little man grown and handsome.	He was a small man in size and handsome.
Hann átti sér bróður er Hreiðar hét.	He had himself a-brother who Hreidar was-named.	He had a brother, who was named Hreidar.
Hann var ljótur maður og varla sjálfbjargi fyrir vits sökum.	He was ugly man and scarcely self-supported for wits sake.	He was an ugly man and he could scarcely take care of himself.
Hann var manna frávastur og vel að afli búinn og hógvær í skapi og var hann heima jafnan.	He was a-man swift and well to strength prepared and humble in character and was he at-home always.	He was a fast man and very strong, and humble in character, and he was always at home.
En Þórður var í förum og var hirðmaður Magnúss konungs og mast vel.	But Thord was in travelling and was court-man Magnus the-king and most well.	But Thord was a travelling man, and a court man of King Magnus who thought most well of him.
Og eitt sinni er Þórður bjó skip sitt í Eyjafirði þá kom Hreiðar þar bróðir hans.	And once his was Thord prepared ship his in Eyjafjord then came Hreidar there brother his.	And one day when Thord was preparing his ship in Eyjafjord, then came Hreidar his brother.
Og er Þórður sá hann spurði hann hví hann væri þar kominn.	And when Thord saw him asked he why he was there coming.	And when Thord saw him, he asked why he had come there.
Hreiðar segir:	Hreidar said:	Hreidar said:
"Eigi nema erindið væri".	"Nothing except errand was".	"I would not have come unless I had business".
"Hvað viltu þá?"	"What will-you then?"	"What do you want then?"
segir Þórður.	said Thord.	said Thord.

The Tale of Hreiðarr the Fool (Old Icelandic)

Old Icelandic	Literal	English
"Eg vil fara utan",	"I wish travel out",	"I wish to travel abroad",
segir Hreiðar.	said Hreidar.	said Hreidar.
Þórður mælti:	Thord spoke:	Thord spoke:
"Ekki þykir mér þér fallin förin.	"Not think I you fallen for-travelling.	"I don't think you are destined for travelling".
Vil eg heldur það til leggja við þig að þú hafir föðurarf okkarn og er það hálfu meira fé en það er eg hefi í förum".	Wish I rather that to let from you that you have inheritance ours and is that half more money than that which I have in trading-voyages".	"I wish rather than to let you go, for you to have our inheritance, and that is more than half the money which I have in trading voyages".
Hreiðar svarar:	Hreidar answered:	Hreidar answered:
"Þá er lítið vit mitt",	"Then would little know me",	"Then I would know little",
segir hann, "ef eg tek þenna fjárskakka til þess að gefa mig svo upp sjálfan og láta þína umsjá og mun þá hver maður draga af mér fé okkað alls eg kann engi forræði þau er nýt eru.	said he, "if I took that uneven-share to this to gave I so up myself and left your guidance and would then every man draw of me money ours all I know no self-control then where used they-are.	he said, "if I took that uneven share, then gave myself up and left your guidance, and then every man would cheat money out of us, and I know no self-control where they are used.
Og era þér þá betra hlut í að eiga ef eg ber á mönnum eða geri eg aðra óvísu þeim er um fé mitt sitja að lokka af mér en eftir það sé eg barður eða meiddur fyrir mínar tilgerðir enda er það sannast í að þér mun torsótt að halda mér eftir er eg vil fara".	And are you then better share in that own if I bear to people or do I other unknown them is about money mine sit that lure off me but after that so is beat or hurt for mine to-do and is that true in that you should difficulty that rather to-me after that I will travel".	And it is better for you to own a share, if I bear to people or do otherwise unknown things to them, those who attend in luring money away from me, but after that I will be beaten or hurt for my deeds, for that is true, that you will have a hard time keeping me, when I want to go".
"Vera kann það",	"Be can that",	"That may be",
segir Þórður, "en get ekki þá um ferð þína fyrir öðrum mönnum".	said Thord, "but mention not then about travel yours before other people".	said Thord, "but don't mention your travel in front of other people".
Því hét hann.	Therefore promised he.	Therefore he promised.

The Tale of Hreiðarr the Fool (Old Icelandic)

Old Icelandic	Literal	English
Og þegar er þeir bræður eru skildir þá segir Hreiðar hverjum er heyra vill að hann ætlar utan að fara með bróður sínum.	And as-soon-as that they brother were parted then told Hreidar everyone that heard would that he intended out to travel with brother his.	And as soon as they had parted, Hreidar told everyone that would hear him, that he intended to travel abroad with his brother.
Og firna allir Þórð um ef hann flytur utan afglapa.	And criticised all Thord about if he transport out fool.	And everyone criticised Thord, if he travel abroad with such a fool.

2

Og er þeir eru búnir sigla þeir í haf og verða vel reiðfara, koma við Björgyn og þegar spyr Þórður eftir konungi og var honum sagt að Magnús konungur var í bænum og hafði skömmu áður komið og vildi eigi láta kæja sig samdægris, þóttist þurfa hvíldar er hann var nýkominn.	And when they were prepared sailed they to sea and became well voyage, came to Bergen and there asked Thord after the-king and was he told that Magnus the-king was in residence and had recently returned come and willed not be-allowed disturbed him same-day, thought needed rest when he was newly-come.	And when they were ready, they sailed to sea and began their voyage well, they came to Bergen, and there Thord asked for the king, and he was told that King Magnus was in residence and had recently returned home and did not wish to be disturbed that day, because he needed rest after newly coming home.
Brátt litu menn Hreiðar að hann var afbragð annarra manna.	Soon noticed people Hreidar that he was stood-out other men.	Soon people noticed Hreidar, that he stood out from other men.
Hann var mikill og ljótur, ómállatur við þá er hann hitti.	He was tall and ugly, chatty with then who he met.	He was tall and ugly, and chatty with whoever he met.
Og snemma um morguninn áður menn væru vaknaðir stendur Hreiðar upp og kallar:	And early about morning before people were woken stood Hreidar up and called:	And early in the morning, before people were awake, Hreidar stood up and called:
"Vaki þú bróðir.	"Wake you brother.	"Wake up, brother.
Fátt veit sá er sefur.	Little knows so who sleeps.	He who sleeps knows little.
Eg veit tíðindi og heyrði eg áðan læti kynleg".	I know news and heard I earlier noise strange".	I have some news, and earlier I heard a strange noise.
"Hverju var líkast?"	"What was like?"	"What was it like?"
spyr Þórður.	asked Thord.	asked Thord.
"Sem yfir kykvendum",	"Like about some-beast",	"Like some beast",

The Tale of Hreiðarr the Fool (Old Icelandic)

Old Icelandic	Literal	English
segir Hreiðar, "og þaut við mjög en aldrei veit eg hvað látum var".	said Hreidar, "and shrill as much but never knew I what have was".	said Hreidar, "and as shrill as one, but I never knew what it was".
"Lát eigi svo undarlega",	"Have not so strange",	"That is not so strange",
segir Þórður.	said Thord.	said Thord.
"Það mun verið hafa hornblástur".	"It must been have trumpet-blast".	"It must have been a blast from a trumpet".
"Hvað skal það tákna?"	"What shall it betoken?"	"What does that mean?"
spyr Hreiðar.	asked Hreidar.	asked Hreidar.
Þórður svarar:	Thord answered:	Thord answered:
"Blásið er jafnan til móts eða til skipdráttar".	"Trumpet-blast is always to meetings or to ship-launching".	"A trumpet blast always means a meeting being summoned or for the launching of ships".
"Hvað táknar mótið?"	"What taken meetings?"	"What are these meetings taken for?"
spyr Hreiðar.	asked Hreidar.	asked Hreidar.
"Þar eru dæmd vandamál jafnan",	"They are to-deem disputes equally",	"They are to judge disputes equally",
segir Þórður, "og slíkt talað sem konungur þykist þurfa að fyrir alþýðu sé upp borið".	said Thord, "and such told as the-king seems needed that before the-people so up bear".	said Thord, "and for things to be told, such as the king sees fit, to bear to the people".
"Hvort mun konungur nú á mótinu?"	"Whether shall the-king now at meeting?"	"Will the king be there now at the meeting?"
spyr Hreiðar.	asked Hreidar.	asked Hreidar.
"Það ætla eg víst",	"That suppose I certainly",	"I suppose so, certainly",
svarar Þórður.	answered Thord.	answered Thord.
"Þangað verð eg þá að fara",	"From-here worth I then to go",	"Then it is worth me going there",

The Tale of Hreiðarr the Fool (Old Icelandic)

Old Icelandic	Literal	English
segir Hreiðar, "því að eg vildi þar koma fyrst er eg sæi sem flesta menn í senn".	said Hreidar, "because that I wish there to-come first that I see as most people to together".	said Hreidar, "because I wish to go there first, to see as many people together at once".
"Þá skýtur í tvö horn með okkur",	"Then throws to two corners with us",	"Then that throws into two corners with us",
segir Þórður.	said Thord.	said Thord.
"Mér þætti því betur er þú kæmir þar síður er fjölmennt væri og vil eg hvergi fara".	"To-me seems therefore better that you come there less when crowded will-be and wish I nowhere to-go".	"It seems better to me therefore that you go there less, when it will be crowded, and I don't wish to go there myself".
"Ekki tjáir slíkt að mæla",	"Not express such to discuss",	"It does not do to say such a thing",
segir Hreiðar, "fara skulum við báðir.	said Hreidar, "travel shall we both.	said Hreidar, "we shall travel both.
Muna þér betra þykja að eg fari einn en ekki færð þú mig lattan þessarar farar".	Should you better to-think that I travel alone and not can you me dissuade this-kind-of journey".	I think you had better realise, that I am going alone, and you can not dissuade me from making this journey".
Hleypur Hreiðar á brott.	Ran Hreidar to away.	Then Hreidar ran away,
En Þórður sér nú að fara mun verða og fer hann eftir er Hreiðar fer hart undan og er mjög langt milli þeirra.	When Thord saw now that going should be also went he after as Hreidar went hard away and was much long between them.	But now Thord saw that this would happen, he also went after him, as Hreidar went hard away, and there was a long way between them.
Og er Hreiðar sér að Þórður fór seint þá mælti hann:	And when Hreidar saw that Thord went slowly then spoke he:	And when Hreidar saw, that Thord was going slowly, then he spoke:
"Það er þó satt, að illt er lítill að vera þá er aflið nær ekki.	"It is though true, that bad is small to be then that strength near is-not.	"It is true that it is bad to be small, because then strength is not near.
En þó mætti vera fráleikurinn en lítið ætla eg þig af honum hafa hlotið.	But though may be swiftness but little suppose I you of it have bound-to.	But though one can still be swift, but I suppose you have little of that,
Og væria þér verri vænleikur minni og kæmist þú með öðrum mönnum".	And be to-you worse handsome less and come you as other men".	and you should be less handsome, and quicker as other men are".

The Tale of Hreiðarr the Fool (Old Icelandic)

Old Icelandic	Literal	English
Þórður svaraði:	Thord answered:	Thord answered:
"Eigi veit eg mér verr fara óknáleik minn en þér afl þitt".	"Not know I me worse to-be prowess mine than you strength yours".	"I do not know if it is worse to have my weakness than your strength".
"Handkrækjumst þá bróðir",	"Hands-hook-us then brother",	"Let us hook hands then, brother",
segir Hreiðar.	said Hreidar.	said Hreidar,
Og nú gera þeir svo, fara um hríð og er svo að Þórði tekur að dofna höndin og lætur hann laust, þykir eigi verða vinveitt að þeir haldist á við álpun Hreiðars.	And now did they so, went about awhile and was seen that Thord took that numb hand and had he let-go, felt not was friendly that they rather that against rough Hreidar.	and so they did, and after a while, and Thord's hand became so numb, that he had to let go, and he felt it was not friendly, because Hreidar was too rough.
Hreiðar fer nú undan svo við fót og nemur stað síðan á hæð nakkvarri og er allstarsýnn, sér þaðan fjölmennið þangað sem mótið var.	Hreidar went now away-from so with foot and took place afterwards to height some and was fixed-upon, saw from-there many-people there as meeting were.	Hreidar now went away and ran, and so it happened afterwards, that he came to a hill and stopped there, he looked from there and saw many people, that were at a meeting.
Og er Þórður kemur eftir mælti hann:	And as Thord came after spoke he:	And as Thord came afterwards, he spoke:
"Förum nú báðir saman bróðir".	"Going now both together brother".	"Let's go both together now, brother".
Og Hreiðar gerir svo.	And Hreidar did so.	And Hreidar did so.

3

Og er þeir koma á þingið kenna margir menn Þórð og fagna honum vel og verður konungur áheyrsli.	And when they came to assembly knew many people Thord and welcomed him well and became the-king to-hear.	And when they came to the assembly, many people knew Thord and welcomed him well, and the king came to hear of him.
Og þegar gengur Þórður fyrir konung og kveður hann vel og tekur konungur blíðlega kveðju hans.	And soon went Thord before the-king and greeted he well and took the-king joyfully greeting his.	And soon Thord went before the king and greeted him well, and the king received his greeting joyfully.

The Tale of Hreiðarr the Fool (Old Icelandic)

Old Icelandic	Literal	English
Þegar skildi með þeim bræðrum er þeir komu til þingsins og verður Hreiðar skauttogaður mjög og færður í reikuð.	When parted with them brothers that they came to their-assembly and became Hreidar roughly much and brought to roughly-handled.	When the brothers parted when they came to the assembly, Hreidar was treated roughly and pushed about.
Hann er málugur og hlær mjög og þykir mönnum ekki að minna gaman að eiga við hann og verður honum nú förin ógreið.	He was talkative and laughed much and thought people not that less fun that had with him and became he now travelling un-passable.	He was talkative and laughed a lot, and people thought it no less fun to tease him, and he now became blocked in the crowd.
Konungur spyr Þórð tíðinda og síðan spyr hann hvað þeirra manna væri í för með honum er hann vildi að til hirðvistar færi með honum".	The-king asked Thord news and then asked he what they people were by travelling with him that he wished that to court-visit bring with him".	The king asked Thord for news, and then he asked, and what people were travelling with him, and whether he wished to join him at court.
"Þar er bróðir minn í för,	"There has brother mine so travelled,	"My brother has also travelled here",
segir Þórður.	said Thord.	said Thord.
"Sá maður mun vel vera",	"Such man should well be",	"Such a man should be well",
segir konungur, "ef þér er líkur".	said the-king, "if you is like".	said the king, "if he is like you".
Þórður segir:	Thord said:	Thord said:
"Ekki er hann mér líkur".	"Not is he me like".	"He is not like me".
Konungur mælti:	The-king spoke:	The king spoke:
"Þó má enn vel vera eða hvað er ólíkast með ykkur?"	"Though may but well be but how is unlike with you?"	"That may be, but now is he not like you?"
Þórður mælti:	Thord spoke:	Thord spoke:
"Hann er mikill maður vexti.	"He is great man grown.	"He is very large.
Hann er ljótur og heldur ósýknlegur, sterkur að afli og lundhægur maður".	He is ugly and behold un-innocent-looking, strong in strength and even-spirit man".	He is ugly, and he appears devious looking, and he is greatly strong, but even spirited".
Konungur mælti:	The-king spoke:	The king spoke:

The Tale of Hreiðarr the Fool (Old Icelandic)

Old Icelandic	Literal	English
"Þó má honum vel vera farið að mörgu".	"Though may he well be going that many-ways".	"He may be well in other ways".
Þórður segir:	Thord said:	Thord said:
"Ekki, ekki var hann kallaður viskumaður á unga aldri".	"Not not was he called wise-man in young age".	"He was not called a wise man in his youth".
"Að því fer eg meir",	"That then go I further",	"Then I go further",
segir konungur, "sem nú er eða hvort má hann sjálfur annast sig?"	said the-king, "as now to but how may he himself take-care-of such?"	said the king, "to how he is now, and how he takes care of himself?"
"Ekki dála er það",	"Not bad is that",	"Not bad",
segir Þórður.	said Thord.	said Thord.
Konungur mælti:	The-king spoke:	The king spoke:
"Hví fluttir þú hann utan?"	"Why brought you him out?"	"Why did you bring him out?"
"Herra",	"Lord",	"Lord",
segir Þórður, "hann á allt hálft við mig en hefir öngar nytjar fjárins og engi afskipti sér veitt um peninga, beiðst þessa eins hlutar að fara utan með mér og þótti mér ósannlegt að eigi réði hann einum hlut þars hann lætur mig mörgum ráða.	said Thord, "he has altogether half with me but has no use of-wealth and none dealings so given about money, best this one's share that travel out with me and thought me untrue that not decide he alone share there he leaves much many advice.	said Thord, "he has half of everything with me, but he has no use of wealth and no interest in money, the only thing he has asked me is to travel abroad with me, and I thought it would be unfair to decide to leave him alone, when he lets me decide so much.
Þótti mér og líklegt að hann mundi gæfu af yður hljóta ef hann kæmi á yðarn fund".	Thought me and favourable that he would be-gifted of your luck if he came to you meet".	I thought it would be favourable and good luck if he came to meet you".
"Sjá vildi eg hann",	"So willed I him",	"So I wish to meet him",
segir konungur.	said the-king.	said the king.
"Svo skal og",	"So shall and",	"So shall it be",
segir Þórður, "en brottu er hann nú rjáður nokkur".	said Thord, "but steep is he now worried somewhat".	said Thord, "but he is now somewhat worried".
Konungur sendi nú eftir honum.	The-king sent now after him.	The king now sent for him.

The Tale of Hreiðarr the Fool (Old Icelandic)

Old Icelandic	Literal	English
Og er Hreiðar heyrði sagt að konungur vildi hitta hann þá gengur hann uppstert mjög og nær á hvað sem fyrir var og var hann því óvanur að konungur hefði beiðst fundar hans.	And when Hreidar heard said that the-king wished meet him then walked he upright much and near to what as before was and was he then unaccustomed to the-king having asked to-meet him.	And when Hreidar heard it said, that the king wished to meet him, then he walked very upright and near to what was before him, and he was then unaccustomed to the king having asked to meet him.
Hann var á þá leið búinn að hann var í hökulbrókum og hafði feld grán yfir sér.	He was that then way dressed that he was in ankle-breeches and had cloak grey over himself.	He was dressed in such a way, that he was wearing ankle-breeches and a grey cloak over him.
Og er hann kemur fyrir konung þá fellur hann á kné fyrir konung og kveður hann vel.	And when he came before the-king then fell he on knees before the-king and greeted him well.	And when he came before the king, he then fell on his knees before the king and greeted him well.
Konungur svaraði honum hlæjandi og mælti:	The-king answered him laughing and spoke:	The king laughed and said:
"Ef þú átt við mig erindi þá mæl þú skjótt slíkt er þú vilt.	"If you have with me business then say you swiftly such as you will.	"If you have business with me, then say as swiftly as you will.
Aðrir eiga enn nauðsyn að tala við mig síðan".	Others have but need to talk with me after".	There are others who need to talk with me afterwards".
Hreiðar segir:	Hreidar said:	Hreidar said:
"Mitt erindi þykir mér skyldast.	"My business think to-me obliged.	"I think my business is more urgent.
Eg vildi sjá þig konungur".	I wished to-see you king".	I wished to see you, king".
"Þykir þér nú vel þá",	"Think you now well then",	"Do you think it well now",
segir konungur, "er þú sérð mig?"	said the-king, "that you saw me?"	said the king, "that you saw me?"
"Vel víst",	"Well certainly",	"Well certainly",
segir Hreiðar, "en eigi þykist eg enn til gjörla sjá þig".	said Hreidar, "but not think I that to completely saw you".	said Hreidar, "but I don't think that I have seen you completely".
"Hvernug skulum við nú þá?"	"Which shall we now then?"	"What shall we do now then?"

The Tale of Hreiðarr the Fool (Old Icelandic)

Old Icelandic	Literal	English
segir konungur,	said the-king,	said the king.
"vildir þú að eg stæði upp?"	"would you that I stand up?"	"Would you like me to stand up?"
Hreiðar svarar:	Hreidar answered:	Hreidar answered:
"Það vildi eg",	"That wish i",	"That I would wish",
segir hann.	said he.	he said.
Konungur mælti er hann var upp staðinn:	The-king spoke then he was up standing:	The king spoke, when he stood up:
"Nú munt þú þykjast gjörla sjá mig mega?"	"Now should-you you consider completely seen me may?"	"Now have you seen me completely?"
"Eigi enn til gjörla",	"Not then to completely",	"Not completely",
segir Hreiðar, "og er nú þó nær hófi".	said Hreidar, "and are now though near measure".	said Hreidar, "but it is now closer".
"Viltu þá",	"Wish-you then",	"Do you wish then",
segir konungur, "að eg leggi af mér skikkjuna?"	said the-king, "that I take off my cloak?"	said the king, "that I take off my cloak?"
"Það vildi eg víst",	"That wish I certainly",	"That I certainly wish",
segir Hreiðar.	said Hreidar.	said Hreidar.
Konungur mælti:	The-king spoke:	The king spoke:
"Við skulum þar þó nokkuð innast til áður um það málið.	"We should there though some do to before about that discuss.	"We should then discuss the matter before doing it.
Þér eruð hugkvæmir margir Íslendingar og veit eg eigi nema þú virðir þetta til ginningar.	You are very-smart many Icelander and know I not except you worth this to mocking.	You Icelanders are very smart, and I do not know, if this is mockery.
Nú vil eg það undan skilja".	Now wish I that away-from understand".	Now I wish to be away from that, you understand".
Hreiðar segir:	Hreidar said:	Hreidar said:

The Tale of Hreiðarr the Fool (Old Icelandic)

Old Icelandic	Literal	English
"Engi er til þess fær konungur að ginna þig eða ljúga að þér".	"None that to this capable king of mocking you or lie to you".	"I am not capable of this, king, of mocking you or lying to you".
Konungur leggur nú af sér skikkjuna og mælti:	The-king laid now off his cloak and spoke:	The king now took off his cloak and poke:
"Hyggðu nú að mér svo vandlega sem þig tíðir".	"Think now that me so closely as you wish".	"Think now that you may see me as closely as you wish".
"Svo skal vera",	"So shall be",	"So it shall be",
segir Hreiðar.	said Hreidar.	said Hreidar.
Hann gengur í hring um konunginn og mælti oft hið sama fyrir munni sér:	He walked in a-ring around the-king and spoke frequently to himself before mouth his:	He walked in a ring around the king and spoke frequently to himself and mumbling:
"Allvel, allvel",	"All-well all-well",	"Splendid, splendid",
segir hann.	said he.	he said.
Konungur mælti:	The-king spoke:	The king spoke:
"Hefir þú nú séð mig sem þú vilt?"	"Have you now seen me as you wish?"	"Have you now seen me as you wish?"
"Að vísu",	"That certainly",	"Certainly"
segir hann.	said he.	he said.
Konungur spurði:	The-king asked:	The king asked:
"Hversu líst þér nú á mig þá?"	"How-so appears to-you now of me then?"	"How do I appear to you now then?"
Hreiðar svarar:	Hreidar answered:	Hreidar answered:
"Ekki hefir Þórður bróðir minn ofsögum frá þér sagt það er vel er".	"Not had Thord brother mine off-said from you said that is well be".	"My brother Thord did not exaggerate when he said of your well being".
Konungur mælti:	The-king spoke:	The king spoke:
"Máttu nokkuð að finna um það er þú sérð nú og það er eigi sé í alþýðu viti?"	"May-you something to find about that which you see now and that is not seen by all-the-people knowing?"	"Can you find something that you see now, that has not been seen by other people?"

The Tale of Hreiðarr the Fool (Old Icelandic)

Old Icelandic	Literal	English
"Ekki vil eg að finna",	"Not wish I to find",	"I do not wish to find",
segir hann, "og ekki má eg þegar því að þannug mundi hver sig kjósa sem þú ert þó að sjálfur mætti ráða".	said he, "and not may I from-there accordingly that thus would each themselves choose as you are though that self may advise".	he said, "and I can not find, because thus would everyone choose to be as you are, if they could".
"Mikinn tekur þú af",	"Great take you of",	"You are taking off",
segir konungur.	said the-king.	said the king.
Hreiðar svarar:	Hreidar answered:	Hreidar answered:
"Háttung er öðrum á þá",	"Risk are others for then",	"It is a risk for others then",
segir hann, "að lofgjarnlega sé við mælt ef þú átt þetta eigi að sönnu sem mér líst á þig og eg sagði áðan".	said he, "that praise-will you of speaking if you that this not that true as to-me appears of you and I said earlier".	he said, "for those who praise you, if it is not true, how you appear to me as I said earlier".
Konungur mælti:	The-king spoke:	The king spoke:
"Finn til nokkuð þó að smátt sé".	"Find to something though that small is".	"Find something, though it is small".
"Það helst þá herra",	"Is rather then lord",	"It is then rather",
segir hann, "að auga þitt annað er litlu því ofar en annað".	said he, "that eye the other is a-little before above the other".	he said, "that one eye is a little above the other".
"Það hefir einn maður fyrr fundið",	"That has one man before found",	"Only one man has noticed that before",
segir konungur, "en sá er Haraldur konungur frændi minn.	said the-king, "and that was Harald the-king kinsman mine.	said the king, "and that was King Harald, my kinsman.
Nú skal jafnmæli með okkur",	Now shall equal-speak with you",	Now I shall equally say of you",
segir konungur.	said the-king.	said the king.
"Skaltu nú standa upp og leggja af þér skikkju og vil eg sjá þig".	"Shall-you now stand up and allow off your cloak and will I see you".	"Stand up and take off your cloak, and I will see you".

The Tale of Hreiðarr the Fool (Old Icelandic)

Old Icelandic	Literal	English
Hreiðar fleygir af sér feldinum og hefir saurgar krummur, - maðurinn hentur mjög og ljótur, - en þvegnar heldur latlega.	Hreidar threw off his cloak and had dirty hands, a-man suited much and ugly, but to-wash rather negligently.	Hreidar threw off his cloak, and he had large dirty hands, suited to such an ugly man, and washed negligently.
Konungur hyggur að honum vandlega.	The-king looked at him closely.	The king looked at him closely.
Og þá mælir Hreiðar:	And then spoke Hreidar:	And then Hreidar spoke:
"Herra",	"Lord",	"Lord",
segir hann, "hvað þykist þú nú mega að mér finna?"	said he, "what think you now may that me find?"	he said, "what do you think you may find?"
Konungur segir:	The-king said:	The king said:
"Það ætla eg að eigi fæðist ljótari maður upp en þú ert".	"That suppose I that not born uglier man up than you are".	"That I suppose that there is not a man born uglier than you".
"Slíkt verður mælt",	"Such becomes spoken",	"This is what is said",
segir Hreiðar.	said Hreidar.	said Hreidar.
"Er nokkuð þá",	"But some then",	"But are there some",
segir hann, "að til fríðinda sé um mig að því sem þú leggur ætlun á?"	said he, "that to good-things see about me that therefore which you have suppose of?"	he said, "good things to see about me, that you might suppose?"
Konungur mælti:	The-king spoke:	The king spoke:
"Það sagði Þórður bróðir þinn að þú værir lundhægur maður".	"That said Thord brother yours of you be tempered-even man".	"That your brother Thord said you are an even-tempered man".
"Það er satt og",	"That is true also",	"That is also true",
sagði Hreiðar, "og þykir mér það illt er svo er".	said Hreidar, "and think me that ill is so to-be".	said Hreidar, "and I think that it is bad to be".
"Þú munt reiðast þó",	"Though shall-you anger though",	"Though one day you will become angry",
sagði konungur.	said the-king.	said the king.
"Mæl heill herra",	"Say whole lord",	"Speak well, lord",

The Tale of Hreiðarr the Fool (Old Icelandic)

Old Icelandic	Literal	English
segir Hreiðar, "eða hve langt mun til þess?"	said Hreidar, "but how long could until this?"	said Hreidar, "but how long could it be until this happens?"
"Eigi veit eg það gjörla",	"Not know I that completely",	"That I do not know completely",
segir konungur, "helst á þessum vetri að því er eg get til".	said the-king, "rather of this winter that since that I guess to".	said the king, "rather some time this winter, if my guess is right".
Hreiðar mælti:	Hreidar spoke:	Hreidar spoke:
"Seg heill sögu".	"Tell a-complete story".	"Tell a complete story".
Konungur mælti:	The-king spoke:	The king spoke:
"Ertu nokkuð hagur?"	"Are-you of-any benefit?"	"Are you any good at anything?"
Hreiðar segir:	Hreidar said:	Hreidar said:
"Aldregi hefi eg reynt, má eg því eigi vita".	"Never have I tried, may I therefore not know".	"I have never tried, and therefore I do not know".
"Til þess þætti þó ekki ólíklegt",	"To this seems though not unlikely",	"It does not seem unlikely"
segir konungur.	said the-king.	said the king.
"Seg heill sögu",	"Tell the-whole story",	"Tell the whole story",
kvað Hreiðar.	said Hreidar.	said Hreidar.
"Svo mun vera jafnt þegar er þú segir það.	"So should be equally then as you say it.	"So shall it be, just as you say.
En veturvistar þættist eg þurfa".	And winter-provisions we-have I need".	And I need winter provisions".
Konungur sagði:	The-king said:	The king said:
"Heimil er mín umsjá.	"Home being mine about.	"My home is so about.
En betur þykir mér þér þar vistin felld vera er heldur er fátt manna".	But better think I you then stay shed be where rather are few people".	But I think it better if you stay in the shed, where there are few people".

The Tale of Hreiðarr the Fool (Old Icelandic)

Old Icelandic	Literal	English
Hreiðar svaraði:	Hreidar answered:	Hreidar answered:
"Svo er það og",	"So is it and",	"So it may be",
segir hann.	said he.	he said.
"En eigi mun svo mannfátt vera að eigi komi það þó upp er mælt verður, allra helst það er hlægi þykir í, en eg maður ekki orðvar og jafnan ber mér mart á góma.	"But not would so people-few be that not come that though up in spoken become, all rather that is ridicule thought in, that I people not discreet and equally carry I many about gums.	"But there would not be so few people, that none came up though, and in speaking something that is a joke, people think I am not discreet, and many people carry this about in their mouths.
Nú kann vera að þeir reiði orð mín fyrir aðra menn og spotti mig og drepi það að ferlegu er eg hefi að gamni eða mæli eg.	Now can be that their anger words mine before other people and small me and kill that to monstrous what I have been amuse or speak i.	Now it may be that they angered my words before other people, and mocked me, and kill me for what I have been amused to speak.
Nú sýnist mér hitt viturlegra að vera heldur hjá þeim er um mig hyggur sem Þórður er bróðir minn þótt þar sé heldur fjölmenni en hinnug þótt menn séu fáir og sé þar engi til umbóta".	Now seems I find wisely to be rather by them that about me think as Thord is brother mine thought then be rather followers-many that there though people as few and as there no-one to put-right".	Now it seems to me the wiser thing to be beside those, who about me consider, such as Thord, my brother, though there are more people there than otherwise and there is no one to put things right".
Konungur mælti:	The-king spoke:	The king spoke:
"Ráð þú þá og farið báðir bræður til hirðarinnar ef ykkur líkar það betur".	"Decide you then and go both brothers to court if you like that better".	"You decide then, and you and your brother can both come to court if you would like that better".
Þegar hljóp Hreiðar á brott er hann heyrði þessi orð konungs og segir hverjum manni er á vill hlýða að hans för hefir allgóð orðið á konungs fund, segir og einkum Þórði bróður sínum að konungur hefir leyft honum að fara til hirðvistar.	Straightaway ran Hreidar to away that he heard these words the-king's and told each of-the-people that from well listened that his going had all-good words from the-king visit, said and especially Thord brother his that the-king had given-leave him to travel to court.	Then Hreidar ran away when he heard the king's words, and told every person who listened, how it had gone with all the good words from his visit to the king, and said especially to his brother Thord, that the king had given them leave to travel to court.
Þá mælti Þórður:	Then spoke Thord:	Then Thord spoke:

The Tale of Hreiðarr the Fool (Old Icelandic)

Old Icelandic	Literal	English
"Bú þig þá sæmilega að klæðum eða vopnum því að það eitt samir og skortir okkur ekki til þess og skipast margir menn vel við góðan búning enda er vandara að búa sig í konungs herbergi en annarstaðar og verður síður athlægi ger af hirðmönnum".	"Prepare you then well-enough with clothes and weapons because that it one in-common and shortage ours not to this and changed many people well with good clothing and is important to dress such as the-king's room than any-other-place and become less the made of court-men".	"Prepare yourself well with clothes and weapons, because there is one thing in common, and we have no shortage in this, and many people are changed by good clothing, and it is important to dress well in the king's room more than any other place, and it will avoid ridicule from the court-men".
Hreiðar svarar:	Hreidar answered:	Hreidar answered:
"Eigi getur þú allnær að eg muni skrúðklæðin á mig láta koma".	"Not get you all-near that I should costly-clothing of me allow coming".	"You will not get anywhere near me coming along wearing fancy clothing".
Þórður mælti:	Thord spoke:	Thord spoke:
"Skerum vaðmál þá til".	"Cut homespun-cloth then to".	"Then you will wear cut homespun cloth".
Hreiðar svarar:	Hreidar answered:	Hreidar answered:
"Nær er það",	"Near is that",	"That would be better",
segir hann.	said he.	he said.
Svo er nú gert við ráð Þórðar og lætur Hreiðar eftir leiðast.	So that now did with advice Thord's and had Hreidar afterwards carried-out.	So now it was done with Thord's advice, and then Hreidar had carried it out.
Hefir hann nú vaðmálsklæði og fágar sig og þykir nú þegar allur annar maður, sýnist nú maður ljótur og greitt vasklegur.	Had he now wadding-clothes and cleaned himself and seemed now already all another man, seemed now a-man ugly and ready-to-serve valiant.	Now he had wadding-clothes and cleaned himself, and he already seemed like a different man, he was still ugly, but now valiant looking.
Svo er þó mót á manninum er þeir Þórður eru með hirðinni að Hreiðar verður í fyrstu fyrir miklum ágang af hirðmönnum og breyttu þeir marga vega orðum við hann og fundu að hann var ómállatur.	So was though against about the-people that they Thord were with court-men that Hreidar became the first before much aggression of court-men and varied they many ways words with him and found that he was talkative.	So it was though, in meeting the people, that with Thord and with the court-men, that Hreidar became singled out for much aggression from the court-me, and there were many ways in which they had words with him, and he was talkative.

The Tale of Hreiðarr the Fool (Old Icelandic)

Old Icelandic	Literal	English
Kom við sem mátti og hentu þeir mikið gaman að því að eiga við hann og var hann jafnan hlæjandi við því er þeir mæltu og lagði hvern þeirra fyrir, svo var hann leikmikill, bæði um mælgina og allra helst - -	Came with how it-may and handed they much fun that because that had with he and was he equally laughing with such that they spoke and had each they before, so was he playful, both about talking and all rather	It became how it may, that they had much fun with him, and he was laughing equally as much with them, with what they said, and with each of them he was playful, both in talking and rather in all things.
En fyrir því að hann var rammur að afli og er þeir finna að hann gefst ekki að grandi þá þvarr það allt af þeim hirðmönnum - - nú með hirðinni.	When for then that he was frame that strength and when they found that he gave not to injury then decreased that all of them court-men now with court	Then when they realised how strong his frame was, and when they found that he did not give in to injury, then the mocking of him decreased with all the court-men.

4

Old Icelandic	Literal	English
Í þetta mund voru þeir báðir konungar yfir landi, Magnús konungur og Haraldur konungur,	In that time were they both kings over the-land, Magnus the-king and Harald the-king,	At that time there were two kings ruling over the land, King Magnus, and King Harald.
en þá höfðu sakar gerst - - hirðmaður Magnúss konungs hafði vegið hirðmann Haralds konungs og var lagður til sáttarfundur að konungar skyldu sjálfir finnast og skipa málinu.	but then had conviction made court-man Magnus's the-king had slain court-man Harald's the-king and was laid to peace-meeting that kings should themselves meet-up and exchange the-matter	But then trouble came when one of Magnus's court-men had slain one of Harald's court-men, and they had a peace meeting, so that the kings themselves could meet up and discuss the matter.
Og er Hreiðar heyrir þetta að Magnús konungur skal fara til móts við Harald konung þá fer hann á fund Magnúss konungs og mælti:	And when Hreidar heard this that Magnus the-king shall travel to meet with Harald the-king then went he to find Magnus the-king and spoke:	And when Hreidar heard this, that King Magnus would travel to meet with King Harald, then he went to find King Magnus and spoke:
"Sá hlutur er",	"So share i",	"So I share",
segir hann, "er eg vildi þig biðja".	said he, "that I wish you to-ask".	he said, "something that I wish to ask you".
"Hver er sá?"	"What is so?"	"What is it?"
sagði konungur.	said the-king	said the king.
Hreiðar mælti:	Hreidar spoke:	Hreidar spoke:

The Tale of Hreiðarr the Fool (Old Icelandic)

Old Icelandic	Literal	English
"Að fara til sáttarfundar.	"To travel to peace-meeting	"To travel to the peace meeting.
Em eg ekki víðförull en mér er mikil forvitni á að sjá tvo konunga senn í einum stað".	Am I not widely-travelled but I am much curious about to see two kings they in one place".	I am not widely travelled, but I am very curious to see two kings in one place".
Konungur svarar:	The-king answered:	The king answered:
"Satt segir þú að þú ert ekki víðförull	"True say you that you are not widely-travelled	"It is true to say that you are not widely travelled.
en þeygi mun eg leyfa þér þessa förina því að ekki er þér fellt að ganga í greipur mönnum Haralds konungs.	but yet-not could I allow you this sacrificing for that not are you falling to go in grasp people Harald's the-king	But I could not allow this, to sacrifice you, if you fall into the grasp of King Harald.
Og beri svo til að þér verði að því ólið eða öðrum og em eg um það hræddur að þá sæki þig heim reiðin er þú langar til en mér þætti best að við bærist".	And bear so to that you became that for unaccompanied or others and am I about that worried that then conviction you home uproar that you long to then me seems best that with bearing".	And so it carries, that if you become separated from the others, I am worried that, then you might be involved in trouble, and then you would become angry, and so it seems best to me, with that in mind".
Hreiðar svarar:	Hreidar answered:	Hreidar answered:
"Nú mæltir þú gott orð.	"Now speak you good words	"Now you speak good words.
Þá skal að vísu fara ef eg veit þess vonir að eg reiðist".	Then shall to certainly travel if I know this custom that I become-angry".	Then I am more certain to travel, if I know that I am accustomed to becoming angry".
Konungur segir:	The-king said:	The king said:
"Muntu fara ef eg leyfi eigi?"	"Shall-you travel if I leave not?"	"Will you travel, if I do not give leave for it?"
Hreiðar svarar:	Hreidar answered:	Hreidar answered:
"Eigi þá síður".	"None then less".	"None the less".
"Ætlar þú að þér muni þvílíkt við mig að eiga sem við Þórð bróður þinn því að þar hefir þú jafnan þitt mál?"	"Suppose you that you would therefore-like with me that have as with Thord brother yours because that there have you always your way?"	"Do you suppose, that you would therefore liken me to that which you have with your brother Thord, because you always have your way?"

The Tale of Hreiðarr the Fool (Old Icelandic)

Old Icelandic	Literal	English
Hreiðar segir:	Hreidar said:	Hreidar said:
"Því öllu betra mun mér við yður að eiga sem þú ert vitrari en hann".	"Because all better would me with you than have as you are wiser than he".	"It would be better with you than with him as you are wiser than he is".
Konungur sér nú að hann mun fara þó að hann banni eða hann fari eigi í hans föruneyti og þykir eigi það best ef hann kemur annarstaðar til föruneytis og þykir þá í reiðingum vera hversu honum eirir ef hann vélir einn um og leyfir honum nú heldur að fara með sér og er Hreiðari fenginn hestur til reiðar.	The-king saw now that he would travel though that he banned either he travelled not in his companionship and thought not that best if he came any-other-place to company and thought then in uproar being how-so he own if he wilful one about and leave him now rather that travel with him and was Hreidar given a-horse to ride	The king saw now that he would travel, even though he had banned him, he would travel outside of his companionship, and he thought it not best if he came into another place's company and there was an uproar, how he would be if he was wilful about something, and had him rather travelling with him, and Hreidar was given a horse to ride.
Og þegar er þeir voru á ferð komnir þá reið hann mjög og ætlaði sér varla hóf um og þraut hestinn undir honum.	And as-soon as they were to travel coming then rode he much and intended himself hardly in-moderation about and faltered the-horse under him	And as soon as they were coming to travel, then he rode hard, and hardly in moderation about, and the horse faltered under him.
Og er konungur verður þess var mælti hann:	And when the-king became this aware spoke he:	And when the king became aware of this, he spoke:
"Nú gefur vel til.	"Now give well to	"Now it is well.
Fylgið nú Hreiðari heim og fari hann eigi".	Follow now Hreidar home and travel he not".	Hreidar is to be followed home and he is not to travel".
Hann segir:	He said:	"He said:
"Eigi heftir þetta ferðina mína þótt hesturinn sé þrotinn.	"Not have this travelling mine thought horse's being ended	"Not having this my journey, though the horse has given out".
Kemur mér til lítils fráleikurinn ef eg fæ eigi fylgt yður".	Came me to little game if I give not follow you".	I would not be a good sportsman, if I could not keep up with you".
Fara þeir nú og lögðu margir fram hjá honum hesta sína og þótti gaman að reyna fráleik hans svo gropasamlega sem hann sjálfur tók á.	Travelled they now and had many from beside him horse his and thought fun to test from-game his so grouped-together as he himself took of	Travelled they now and many brought their horses beside his and thought it fun to test his sport. And so grouped together as he took them on.

The Tale of Hreiðarr the Fool (Old Icelandic)

Old Icelandic	Literal	English
En svo gafst að hann þreytti hvern hest er frammi var lagður og lést eigi verður að koma til fundarins ef hann gæti eigi fylgt þeim.	But so gave that he tired each horse that from was had and let not were to come to the-meeting if he got not follow them	But it so happened that he tired each horse, that was laid before him, and he was not to come to the meeting if he could not follow pace with them.
Og fyrir þetta sátu nú margir af sínum hestum.	And ahead that sat now many of his horses	And for this many of their horses now sat.

5

Old Icelandic	Literal	English
Og er þeir koma þar er konungar skulu finnast þá mælti Magnús konungur við Hreiðar:	And when they came there that the-kings shall meet then spoke Magnus the-king with Hreidar:	And when they came to where the kings were to meet, then King Magnus said to Hreidar:
"Ver þú mér nú fylgjusamur og ver á aðra hönd mér og skilst ekki frá mér.	"Be you me now follow-same and be on other hand mine and separate not from me	"Be obedient to me now and me on my other side and do not part with me"
En miðlung segir mér hugur um hversu fer þá er menn Haralds konungs koma og sjá þig".	But poorly say me think about how-so goes then when men Harald's the-king come and see you".	But I think that it will go badly, when King Harald's men come and see you".
Hreiðar kvað svo vera skyldu sem konungur mælti "og þykir mér því betur er eg geng yður nær".	Hreidar spoke so be should as the-king spoke "and think me then better that I go you near".	Hreidar said that it should be as the king said, "and then I think it better that I go nearer to you".
Nú finnast konungar og ganga þeir á tal og ræða mál sín.	Now met the-kings and went they to talk and discuss matters theirs	Now the kings met, and they talked and discussed their matters.
En menn Haralds konungs gátu líta hvar Hreiðar gekk og höfðu heyrt getið hans og þótti þeim um hið vænsta.	When men Harald's the-king got company where Hreidar went and had heard told he and thought they about that good	But King Harold's men could see where Hreidar went, and they had heard his name, and they thought it good.
Og er konungar töluðu þá gengur Hreiðar í flokk Haralds manna og höfðu þeir hann til skógar er skammt var þaðan, skauttoguðu hann mjög og hrundu honum stundum.	And as the-kings talked then went Hreidar in group Harald's men and had they he to woods which short-distance was from-there, pull-cloak, handle-roughly he much and teased him awhile	And when the kings were talking, Hreidar went into the company of Harold's men, and they took him to a forest, which was not far from there, they rough-handled him a lot, and sometimes knocked him down.
En þar lék á ýmsu.	But then played about variously	But they played at him in various ways.

The Tale of Hreiðarr the Fool (Old Icelandic)

Old Icelandic	Literal	English
Stundum fauk hann fyrir sem vindli en stundum var hann fastur fyrir sem veggur og hrutu þeir frá honum.	Sometimes drifted he before as wind then sometimes was he secure before as a-wall and fell they away-from him	Sometimes he drifted before them like the wind, and sometimes he was as secure as a wall, and they fell away from him.
Nú dregst þó svo leikurinn að þeir gera honum nakkvað harðleikið, létu ganga honum öxarsköft og skálpana og námu naddar af sverðskónum í höfði honum og skeindist hann af og svo lét hann sem honum þætti hið mesta gaman að og hló við jafnan.	Now drawn though so the-game that they did him some hardness, had going him axe-handles and scabbards and took studded of sword-studded at head him and scratched he of and so had he as him seemed the most game that and laughed with equally	And as the game drew on, they became hard and were going at him with axe handles and scabbards, and a studded sword scabbard hit him on the head, and scratched him, and he appeared to enjoy the game and laughed equally with them.
Og er svo hafði fram farið um hríð þá tók leikurinn ekki að batna af þeirra hendi.	And was so had from going about awhile then took the-game not to better of them hand	And when this had been going on for a while, the game did not begin to get any better from them.
Þá mælti Hreiðar:	Then spoke Hreidar:	Then Hreidar spoke:
"Nú höfum vér átt góðan leik um stund og er nú ráð að hætta því að nú tekur mér að leiðast.	"Now have we had good sport about awhile and am-i now decide that conclude therefore that now take me to hand	"How we have had good sport for a while, and I have now decided that it shall conclude, therefore take my hand.
Förum nú til konungs yðvars og vil eg sjá hann".	Go now to king yours and will I see him".	Let's go now to your king, and I will see him.
"Það skal verða aldrei",	"That shall be never",	"That shall never be",
sögðu þeir, "svo fjandlegur sem þú ert, að þú skulir sjá konung vorn og skulum vér færa þig til heljar".	said they, "so fiendish as you are, that you should see the-king ours and shall we bring you to death".	they said, "so fiendish as you are, that you should see our king, and we shall bring you to death".
Honum finnst þá fátt um og þykist sjá að það mun fram fara og er nú þar komið að honum rennur í skap og reiðist hann, fer höndum þann mann er mest sótti að honum og verst lék við hann og vegur á loft og færði niður að höfðinu svo að heilinn var úti og er sá dauður.	He found then little about and thought seemed that it would from go and that now there came that he run of mood and angered he, went seized then man the most took with him and worse played with he and proceeded to lift and brought down on head so that brain was out and was so dead	He found that he did not like this at all, and where it seemed it would go, and then it happened, that his mood changed, and he became very angry, he seized the man who had taunted him the worst, and proceeded to lift him up and bring him down on his head, so that his brains came out, and he was dead.

The Tale of Hreiðarr the Fool (Old Icelandic)

Old Icelandic	Literal	English
Nú þykir þeim hann trautt mennskur maður að afli og stukku þeir nú í víginu, fara og segja Haraldi konungi að drepinn var hirðmaður hans.	Now thought they he scarcely human man that strength and leapt they now from the-slaying, went and told Harald the-king that killed was court-man his	Now they thought that he was scarcely human with that strength, and they leapt away from the slaying and told King Harald, that one of his courtmen had been killed.
Konungur svarar:	The-king answered:	The king answered:
"Drepið þann þá er það hefir unnið".	"Kill he then who this has done".	"Kill him then, the one who has done this".
"Eigi er það enn hægra",	"Not is that then easy",	"That is not easy",
segja þeir,	said they,	they said.
"hann er nú í brottu".	"he is now to away".	"He has now gone away".
Það er nú frá Hreiðari að segja að hann hittir Magnús konung.	That is now from Hreidar to say that he found Magnus the-king	It is now said of Hreidar that he met King Magnus.
Konungur mælti:	The-king spoke:	The king spoke:
"Veistu nú hvernug það er að reiðast?"	"Know-you now how that is that anger?"	"Now do you know how your anger is?"
"Já",	"Yes",	"Yes",
segir hann, "nú veit eg".	said he, "now know i".	he said, "now I know".
"Hvernug þótti þér?"	"How thought you?"	"What did you think of it?"
segir konungur,	said the-king,	said the king?
"hitt fann eg að þér var forvitni á".	"it found I that you were curious to".	"I found it that you were curious about it".
Hreiðar svarar:	Hreidar answered:	Hreidar answered:
"Illt þótti mér",	"Badly thought i",	"I thought it bad",
segir hann,	said he,	he said,
"þess var eg fúsastur að drepa þá alla".	"this was I wished to kill then all".	"This was my wish, to then kill them all".
Konungur mælti:	The-king spoke:	The king spoke:

The Tale of Hreiðarr the Fool (Old Icelandic)

Old Icelandic	Literal	English
"Það kom mér jafnt í hug",	"That came to-me equally in thought",	"The same thing came to my thoughts",
segir konungur, "að þú mundir illa reiður verða.	said the-king, "that you would badly angry become	said the king, "that you would become bad when angry.
Nú vil eg senda þig á Upplönd til Eyvindar, lends manns míns, að hann haldi þig fyrir Haraldi konungi	Now will I send you to Uplands to Eyvind, land man mine, that he hold you from Harald the-king	Now I will send you to Uplands to Eyvind, a land man of mine, so that he protects you from King Harald.
því að eg treystist eigi að þín verði gætt ef þú ert með hirðinni, því að vér finnumst, en Haraldur frændi er brögðóttur og er vant við að sjá.	because that I we-trust not that you become taken-care-of if you are with court-men, because that we find, that Harald's kinsmen are tricky and are difficult with to see	I do not trust that you will be taken care of if you are with the court-men, because we find Harald's kinsmen are tricky, and difficult to see.
Kom þá aftur til mín er eg sendi eftir þér".	Come then back to me when I send after you".	Then come back to me, when I send for you".
Nú fer Hreiðar í brott uns hann kemur á Upplönd og tekur Eyvindur við honum eftir orðsending konungs.	Now went Hreidar to away until he came to Uplands and took Eyvind with him after message the-king's	Now Hreidar went away, until he came to Uplands, and Eyvind received him as per the king's message.
Konungar höfðu sáttir orðið á það mál er áður var milli þeirra og var því sætt.	The-kings had agreed words of the matter that before was between them and was therefore settled	The kings had agreed words about the matter, which was between them, and it was therefore settled.
En hér verða þeir eigi ásáttir.	But here became they not place-about	But here they became not in agreement.
Þykir Magnúsi konungi þessir menn hafa sjálfir fyrirgert sér og valdið öllum sökum og þykir hirðmaður fallið hafa óheilagur	Thought Magnus the-king these men had themselves fore-done him and wielded all blame and thought court-man fallen had unholy	Magnus thought that these men had forgiven themselves and wielded all the blame, and thought that the court-man had fallen unholy.
en Haraldur konungur beiðir bóta fyrir hirðmann sinn og skildust nú með öngri sætt.	then Harald the-king asked compensation for court-man his and separated now with no settlement	But King Harald begged compensation for his court-man, and now they parted with no settlement.

The Tale of Hreiðarr the Fool (Old Icelandic)

Old Icelandic	Literal	English
6	**6**	**6**
Eigi liðu langar stundir áður Haraldur konungur spyr hvar Hreiðar er niður kominn, gerir síðan ferð sína og kemur á Upplönd til Eyvindar, hefir með sér sex tigu manna.	Not passed long while before Harald the-king learned where Hreidar then down came, made afterwards travelled he and came to Uplands to Eyvind, had with him six tens men	Not a long while had passed, before King Harald learned where Hreidar had come down to, and went afterwards to travel and come to Uplands to Eyvind, having with him sixty men.
Hann kemur þar um morgun snemma og ætlaði að koma á óvart.	He came there about morning early and intended to come to un-warned	He came there early in the morning and intended to come without warning.
En það var þó eigi því að Eyvindur þóttist vita fyrir að hann mundi koma og var hann á öngri stundu vanbúinn við.	But that was though not therefore that Eyvind thought knowing before that he would come and was he that no time unprepared against	But that was not to be, because Eyvind had thought before that he knew that he would come, and at no time was he unprepared against this.
Hafði hann stefnt liði að sér af launungu og var það í skógum þeim er nálægir voru bænum.	Had he located company that he of secretly and was that in the-woods they were near-lying were dwelling	He had located a company secretly, and they were in the woods, lying near the dwelling.
Skyldi Eyvindur gefa þeim mark ef Haraldur konungur kæmi og þóttist hann liðs þurfa.	Should Eyvind give them sign if Harald the-king came and thought he company needed	And Eyvind was to give them a sign, if King Harald came, and if he thought he needed company.
Það er sagt einhverju sinni áður Haraldur konungur kæmi að Hreiðar beiddist að Eyvindur skyldi fá honum silfur og nokkuð gull.	It was said once this after Harald the-king came that Hreidar asked that Eyvind should get him silver and some gold	It was said that once King Harald had arrived, Hreidar asked Eyvind to get him silver and some gold.
"Ertu hagur?"	"Are-you handy?"	"Are you handy?"
segir hann.	said he	he said.
Hreiðar svarar:	Hreidar answered:	Hreidar answered:
"Það sagði Magnús konungur mér.	"That said Magnus the-king to-me	"King Magnus said that to me.
En eigi má ég annað til vita því að ég hefi aldrei við leitað.	But not may I other to know because that I have never with sought	But I must know nothing else, for I have never sought.

The Tale of Hreiðarr the Fool (Old Icelandic)

Old Icelandic	Literal	English
En því mundi hann það segja að hann mundi vita og því trúi eg er hann sagði".	But because should he that say that he would know and therefore trust I what he said".	But because he said that, he should know, and therefore I trust what he said".
Eyvindur mælti:	Eyvind spoke:	Eyvind spoke:
"Þú ert undarlegur maður",	"You are a-strange man",	"You are a strange man",
segir hann,	said he,	he said.
"nú mun eg fá þér efnin.	"now should I give you materials	"Now should I get you the materials.
Skaltu fá mér silfrið ef ónýtt verður smíðað en njót sjálfur ellegar".	Shall-you get me silver if ruined becomes made then enjoy yourself otherwise".	You shall get silver from me, but if the construction becomes ruined, give it back to me, if not, enjoy yourself".
Hreiðar er byrgður í einu húsi og er hann þar að smíðinni.	Hreidar then closed in a house and was he there to smith	Hreidar was then kept in a house, and he began there his smithery.
Og áður en gert verði það er Hreiðar smíðaði þá kemur Haraldur konungur og er nú sem eg gat áður að Eyvindur er að öngu óbúinn og gerir hann konungi veislu góða.	And before then made was that which Hreidar making then came Harald the-king and was now as I got before that Eyvind was that none unprepared and made he the-king feast good	And before Hreidar finished what he was making, then came King Harald, and it was now as said before, that Eyvind was not unprepared, and he made the king a good feast.
Og nú er þeir sitja í drykkju þá fréttir konungur eftir ef Hreiðar sé þar - "og muntu hafa vináttu af mér í móti ef þú selur oss manninn".	And now were they sitting to drinking then news the-king afterwards of Hreidar seeing there "and shall-you have friendship of me in meeting if you sell us the-man".	And now when they were sitting drinking, then the King heard that Hreidar had been seen there, "and you shall have my friendship meeting if you sell us the man".
Eyvindur svarar:	Eyvind answered:	Eyvind answered:
"Eigi er hann hér nú",	"Not is he here now",	"He is not here now".
segir hann.	said he.	he said.
"Eg veit",	"I know",	"I know",
segir konungur, "að hann er og þarftu eigi dylja".	said the-king, "that he is and need-you not disguise".	said the king, "that he is, and you need not disguise it".
Eyvindur mælti:	Eyvind spoke:	Eyvind spoke:

The Tale of Hreiðarr the Fool (Old Icelandic)

Old Icelandic	Literal	English
"En þótt það sé þá geri eg eigi þann mun ykkar Magnúss konungs að eg selji þann mann í hendur þér er hann vill skýla láta", - gekk út síðan úr stofunni.	"But though that he then do I not then would you Magnus the-king that I sell then that-man in hand you then he will protect be", went out afterwards out-of the-room	"Even though he is, then I would not then betray King Magnus by selling that man to you and handing over the man he wishes to be protected", and with that he went out of the room.
Og er hann kemur út þá brýst Hreiðar á hurðina og kallar að hann vill á brott.	And when he came out then hammering Hreidar to-the-door and called that he wished to away	And when he came out, then Hreidar began hammering on the door and calling that he wished to get out.
"Þegi þú",	"Silent you",	"Be quiet",
segir Eyvindur.	said Eyvind.	said Eyvind.
"Haraldur konungur er hér kominn og vill drepa þig".	"Harald the-king is here come and wishes to-kill you".	"King Harald has come here and he wishes to kill you".
Hreiðar brýst út eigi að síður og lést hitta vildu konung.	Hreidar hammering out not the less and let meet wiled the-king	Hreidar hammered on the door no less, and wished to meet the king.
Eyvindur sér þá að hann mun brjóta upp hurðina, gengur til og lýkur upp og mælti:	Eyvind himself then that he would break up the-door, going to and concluded up and spoke:	Eyvind saw then that he was going to break open the door, and went and unlocked it and said:
"Gramir munu taka þig",	"Anger shall take you",	"Anger shall take you",
segir hann, "er þú gengur til banans".	said he, "then you go to death".	he said, "then you go to your death".
Hreiðar gengur inn í stofuna og fyrir konung og kveður hann og mælti:	Hreidar went in to the-room and before the-king and spoke he and said:	Hreidar went into the room and before the king and spoke to him and said:
"Herra tak af mér reiðina því að eg em þér vel felldur fyrir margs sakir að gera það er þú vilt gera láta þó að eigi sé allríflegt í mannraunum eða því er við ber og mun eg þess ólatur er þú vilt mig til hafa sendan.	"Lord take off me anger because that I am to-you well situated for many reasons to do that which you wish done have though that not is all-abundant in human-trials or otherwise is with carrying and should I this not-forget when you wish me to have sent	"Lord, do not be angry with me, because I am pleased to do that which you wish to have done, even though it may not seem rich in human trials or so carried with, and I will not forget it, when you will have me sent for.

The Tale of Hreiðarr the Fool (Old Icelandic)

Old Icelandic	Literal	English
Hér er nú gripur er eg vil gefa þér", - setur á borðið fyrir hann en það var svín gert af silfri og gyllt.	Here is now treasure that I wish to-give you", set on table before him then that was a-pig made of silver and gold	Here is now a treasure, that I wish to give you", he set it on the table before him, and it was a pig made of silver and gold.
Þá mælti konungur er hann leit á svínið:	Then spoke the-king that he looked at the-pig:	Then the king spoke when he looked at the-pig:
"Þú ert hagur svo að trautt hefi eg séð jafnvel smíðað með því móti sem er".	"You are skilled so that scarcely have I seen equally-well smithery with this of such as".	"You are so skilled, that scarcely have I seen such craftsmanship as this".
Nú fer það með manna höndum.	Now passed that among the-men handed	Now it passed among people's hands.
Segir konungur að hann mun taka sættir af honum - "og er gott að senda þig til stórvirkja.	Said the-king that he would take settle of him "and was god that sending you to great-work	The king said that he would he would take settlement with him, "and it would be good to send you on great work.
Þú ert maður sterkur og ófælinn að því er eg hygg".	You are a-man strong and without-fear that therefore am I minded".	You are a strong man and without fear, and therefore I am minded".
Nú kemur svínið aftur fyrir konung.	Now came the-pig before in-front-of the-king	Now came the pig back to the king.
Tekur hann þá upp og hyggur að smíðinni enn vandlegar og sér þá að spenar eru á og það var gyltur, fleygir þegar í brott og sér að til háðs var gert og mælti:	Took he then up and considered that the-work then carefully and saw then that suckling was then and that was young-sow, threw then to away and he that to mockery was done and spoke:	He then picked it up and looked at the work then carefully, and then he saw that the pig was a suckling and a young-sow, then he threw it away, because he believed that it insulted him, and he spoke:
"Hafi þig allan tröll.	"Have you all monstrous	"Have you all, the devil.
Standi menn upp og drepi hann".	Stand men up and kill him".	Stand up men and kill him".
En Hreiðar tekur svínið og gengur út og fer þegar á brott þaðan og kom á fund Magnúss konungs og segir honum hvað í hefir gerst.	Then Hreidar took the-pig and went away and travelled straightaway to away from-there and came to meet Magnus the-king and told him what so had done	Then Hreidar took the pig, went away and travelled straightaway from there to meet King Magnus and told him how it had gone.

The Tale of Hreiðarr the Fool (Old Icelandic)

Old Icelandic	Literal	English
En í öðru lagi standa menn upp og út eftir honum og ætla drepa hann	Then with others lead standing men up and out after him and intended kill him	Then the others stood up and went out after him intending to kill him.
og er þeir koma út þá er Eyvindur þar fyrir og hefir fjölmenni mikið svo að ekki máttu þeir eftir Hreiðari halda og skilja þeir Eyvindur og Haraldur konungur við svo búið og líkar konungi illa.	and when they came out then was Eyvind there before and had followers many so that not may they after Hreidar held and parted they Eyvind and Harald the-king with so settled and liked the-king badly	And when they came outside, then Eyvind was there with many followers, so they could not go after Hreidar. Then Eyvind and King Harald parted, and the king was far from pleased.
Og er þeir hittast Magnús konungur og Hreiðar fréttir konungur eftir hvernug farið hefir.	And when they met Magnus the-king and Hreidar news the-king after how fared had	And when they met, King Magnus and Hreidar, the king asked for news of how it had gone.
En Hreiðar segir frá hið sanna og sýnir konungi svínið.	Then Hreidar told from the truth and showed the-king the-pig	Then Hreidar told the truth about what happened and showed the king the pig.
Magnús konungur mælti þá er hann hugði að svíninu:	Magnus the-king spoke then that he thought that the-pig:	King Magnus then spoke and said that he thought that the pig was:
"Geysihaglega er þetta smíðað	"Exceedingly-skilful was that crafted	"Exceedingly skilfully crafted.
en hefnt hefir Haraldur konungur frændi vor mjög minni háðungar en í þessu er og eigi ertu alláræðislítill og þó með öllu hugkvæmur".	but revenge had Harald the-king kinsman ours much less insult than in this has and not are-you very-timid and though with all ingenuity".	But King Harald, our kinsman, had revenge for much less of an insult than this, and you are not at all timid and though you are full of ingenuity".

7

Hreiðar var nú þar nakkvara stund með Magnúsi konungi.	Hreidar was now there some time with Magnus the-king	Hreidar was now there some time with Magnus the-king.
Og eitthvert sinn kemur hann að máli við konung og mælti:	And one occasion came he to speak with the-king and spoke:	And on one occasion he came to speak with the king and said:
"Það vildi eg konungur að þú veittir mér það er eg mun biðja þig".	"It wish I king that you grant me that which I may ask you".	"It is my wish, king, that you grant me that which I ask you".
"Hvað er það?"	"What is that?"	"What is that?"

The Tale of Hreiðarr the Fool (Old Icelandic)

Old Icelandic	Literal	English
spyr konungur.	asked the-king	asked the-king.
"Það herra",	"That lord",	"That, lord",
segir Hreiðar, "að þér hlýdduð kvæði er eg hefi ort um yður".	said Hreidar, "that you listen-to poem that I have worded about you".	said Hreidar, "that you listen-to poem, that I have worded about you".
"Hví skal eigi það?"	"Why should not that?"	"Why should not that?"
segir konungur.	said the-king	said the-king.
Nú kveður Hreiðar kvæðið og er það allundarlegt, fyrst kynlegast en því betra er síðar er.	Now recited Hreidar the-poem and was it all-wonderful, first strangely then since better then afterwards was	Now Hreidar recited the poem, and it was all wonderful, strange at first, but then it got better after that.
Og er lokið er kvæði mælti konungur:	And when ended was the-poem spoke the-king:	And when the poem had ended, the king spoke:
"Þetta kvæði sýnist mér undarlegt og þó gott að nestlokum.	"That poem seems to-me wonderful and though good as the-end	"That poem seems to be to be wonderful, particularly good at the end.
En kvæðið mun vera með þeim hætti sem ævi þín.	Then poem should be with the way as life yours	Then the poem should be the same way as your life.
Hún hefir fyrst verið með kynlegu móti og einrænlegu en hún mun þó vera því betur er meir líður á.	It has first been with strange meeting and eccentric but it shall though become therefore better the more passes so	First it has been strange and eccentric, but it shall become better the more passes.
Hér eftir skal eg og velja kvæðislaunin.	Here after shall I and will poem-reward	Here after I shall give you a poem's reward.
Hér er hólmur einn fyrir Noregi sá er eg vil þér gefa.	Here is small-island one along Norway so that I will you give	Here is a small island along Norway, so I will give it to you.
Hann er með góðum grösum og er það gott land þó að eigi sé mikið".	It is with good grass and is that good land though is not so large".	It is good with grass, and good land, though it is not so large".
Hreiðar mælti:	Hreidar spoke:	Hreidar spoke:
"Þar skal eg samtengja með Noreg og Ísland".	"There shall I unite with Norway and Iceland".	"There shall I unite with Norway and Iceland".
Konungur mælti:	The-king spoke:	The king spoke:

The Tale of Hreiðarr the Fool (Old Icelandic)

Old Icelandic	Literal	English
"Eigi veit eg hversu það fer.	"One-thing know I how-so that goes	"I know one thing about how it goes.
Hitt veit eg að margir menn munu búnir að kaupa að þér hólminn og gefa þér fé fyrir	This know I that many people shall offer to buy of you the-island and give you fee for	This I know, that many people shall offer to buy the island from you and give you wealth for.
en ráðlegra ætla eg vera að eg leysi til mín að eigi verði að bitbeini þér eða þeim er kaupa vilja.	but advisable suppose I be that I redeem to me that not becomes a bite-bone to-you or they who buy wish-to	But. I advise you to sell the island to me, so that it does not become a bone of contention to you, or those who wish to buy it.
Er nú og ekki vel felld vist þín vilgis lengi hér í Noregi því að eg þykist sjá hvern Haraldur konungur vill þinn hlut ef hann á að ráða sem hann mun ráða ef þú ert lengi í Noregi".	Then now also I well end hospitality yours very long here in Norway because that I think so who Harald the-king will your matter if he has the decision as he shall decide if you are long in Norway".	Then I will also end your very long stay here in Norway, because I think that King Harald will do to you, if he gets the chance, and he shall do what he wants if you stay here much longer".
Nú gaf Magnús konungur honum silfur fyrir hólminn og vill nú eigi þar hætta honum og fór Hreiðar út til Íslands og bjó norður í Svarfaðardal þar sem síðan heitir á Hreiðarsstöðum og gerist mikill maður fyrir sér.	Now gave Magnus the-king him silver for the-island and wished now not there endanger him and travelled Hreidar out to Iceland and settled north in Svarfardal there which afterwards is-named by Hreidar's-Place and became a-great man before himself	Now King Magnus gave him silver for the island and wished that he now not endanger himself, and Hreidar travelled to Iceland and settled north in Svarfardal, which was afterwards named Hreidar's Place, and he became a great man before himself.
Og fer hans ráð mjög eftir getu Magnúss konungs að þess betur er er meir líður fram hans ævi og hefir hann gert sér að mestum hluta þau kynjalæti er hann sló á sig hinn fyrra hlut ævinnar.	And went his advised much after could Magnus the-king that this better was that more passed from his life and had he done himself the most share then eccentricities that he struck to himself the last-years share of-life	And his life went much as King Magnus had advised, that his life would get better the more it passed, for he had made up for the greater share of eccentricities that he inflicted on himself in the first part of his life.
Bjó hann til elli í Svarfaðardal og eru margir menn frá honum komnir.	Lived he to old-age in Svarfardal and are many people from him coming	He lived to old age in Svarfardale and many people are descended from him.
Og lýkur hér þessi ræðu.	And concluded here this speech	And here this speech is concluded.

Word List (Old Icelandic to English)

Old Icelandic	English
A, a	
að	a, as, at, been, in, is, of, on, than, that, the, to, with
aðra	other
aðrir	others
af	of, of, off
afbragð	stood-out
afglapa	fool
afl	strength
afli	strength
aflið	strength
afskipti	dealings
aftur	back, before
aldregi	never
aldrei	never, never
aldri	age
alla	all
allan	all
alláræðislítill	very-timid
allgóð	all-good
allir	all
allnær	all-near
allra	all, all
allríflegt	all-abundant
alls	all
allstarsýnn	fixed-upon
allt	all, altogether
allundarlegt	all-wonderful
allur	all
allvel	all-well
allvel,	all-well
alþýðu	all-the-people, the-people
annað	other, other
annar	another
annarra	other
annarstaðar	any-other-place
annast	take-care-of
athlægi	the
auga	eye
Á, á	
á	about, at, by, for, from, has, in, of, on, so, that, then, to
áðan	earlier
áður	after, before, returned
ágang	aggression
áheyrsli	to-hear
álpun	rough
ásáttir	place-about
átt	had, have, that
átti	had
Æ, æ	
ætla	intended, suppose
ætlaði	intended
ætlar	intended, suppose
ætlun	suppose
ævi	life
ævinnar	of-life
B, b	
báðir	both
bæði	both
bænum	dwelling, residence
bærist	bearing
banans	death
banni	banned
barður	beat
batna	better
beiddist	asked
beiðir	asked
beiðst	asked, best
ber	bear, carry, carrying
beri	bear
best	best
betra	better

Word List (Old Icelandic to English)

Old Icelandic	English
betur	better
biðja	ask, to-ask
bitbeini	bite-bone
bjó	lived, prepared, settled
Björgyn	Bergen
blásið	trumpet-blast
blíðlega	joyfully
borðið	table
borið	bear
bóta	compensation
bræðrum	brothers
bræður	brother, brothers
brátt	soon
breyttu	varied
brjóta	break
bróðir	brother
bróður	a-brother, brother
brögðóttur	tricky
brott	away
brottu	away, steep
brýst	hammering
bú	prepare
búa	dress
búið	settled
búinn	dressed, prepared
búning	clothing
búnir	offer, prepared
byrgður	closed

D, d

dæmd	to-deem
dála	bad
dauður	dead
dofna	numb
draga	draw
dregst	drawn
drepa	kill, to-kill
drepi	kill
drepið	kill
drepinn	killed
drykkju	drinking
dylja	disguise

E, e

Old Icelandic	English
eða	and, but, either, or
ef	if, of
efnin	materials
eftir	after, afterwards
eg	i, is
eiga	had, have, own
eigi	none, not, nothing, one-thing
einhverju	once
einkum	especially
einn	alone, one
einrænlegu	eccentric
eins	one's
einu	a
einum	alone, one
eirir	own
eitt	once, one
eitthvert	one
ekki	i, is-not, not
ekki,	not
ellegar	otherwise
elli	old-age
em	am
en	and, but, than, that, the, then, when
enda	and
engi	no, none, no-one
enn	but, that, then
er	am, am-i, are, as, be, being, but, has, i, in, is, that, the, then, to, to-be, was, were, what, when, where, which, who, whom, would
era	are
erindi	business
erindið	errand
ert	are
ertu	are-you
eru	are, they-are, was, were
eruð	are
Eyjafirði	Eyjafjord

Word List (Old Icelandic to English)

Old Icelandic	English
Eyvindar	Eyvind
Eyvindur	Eyvind

F, f

Old Icelandic	English
fá	get, give
fæ	give
fæðist	born
fær	capable
færa	bring
færð	can
færði	brought
færður	brought
færi	bring
fágar	cleaned
fagna	welcomed
fáir	few
fallið	fallen
fallin	fallen
fann	found
fara	go, going, to-be, to-go, travel, travelled, went, went
farar	journey
fari	travel, travelled
farið	fared, go, going
fastur	secure
fátt	few, little
fauk	drifted
fé	fee, money
feld	cloak
feldinum	cloak
felld	end, shed
felldur	situated
fellt	falling
fellur	fell
fenginn	given
fer	go, goes, passed, travelled, went
ferð	travel, travelled
ferðina	travelling
ferlegu	monstrous
finn	find
finna	find, found
finnast	meet, meet-up, met
finnst	found
finnumst	find
firna	criticised
fjandlegur	fiendish
fjárins	of-wealth
fjárskakka	uneven-share
fjölmenni	followers, followers-many
fjölmennið	many-people
fjölmennt	crowded
flesta	most
fleygir	threw
flokk	group
fluttir	brought
flytur	transport
föðurarf	inheritance
fór	travelled, went
för	going, travelled, travelling
förin	for-travelling, travelling
förina	sacrificing
forræði	self-control
förum	go, going, trading-voyages, travelling
föruneyti	companionship
föruneytis	company
forvitni	curious
fót	foot
frá	away-from, from
frændi	kinsman, kinsmen
fráleik	from-game
fráleikurinn	game, swiftness
fram	from
frammi	from
frávastur	swift
fréttir	news
fríðinda	good-things
fund	find, meet, visit
fundar	to-meet
fundarins	the-meeting
fundið	found
fundu	found
fúsastur	wished
fylgið	follow
fylgjusamur	follow-same

Word List (Old Icelandic to English)

Old Icelandic	English
fylgt	follow
fyrir	ahead, along, before, for, from, in-front-of
fyrirgert	fore-done
fyrr	before
fyrra	last-years
fyrst	first
fyrstu	first

G, g

Old Icelandic	English
gæfu	be-gifted
gæti	got
gætt	taken-care-of
gaf	gave
gafst	gave
gaman	fun, game
gamni	amuse
ganga	go, going, went
gat	got
gátu	got
gefa	gave, give, to-give
gefst	gave
gefur	give
gekk	went
geng	go
gengur	go, going, walked, went
ger	made
gera	did, do, done
geri	do
gerir	did, made
gerist	became
gerst	done, made
gert	did, done, made
get	guess, mention
getið	told
getu	could
getur	get
geysihaglega	exceedingly-skilful
ginna	mocking
ginningar	mocking
gjörla	completely
Glúmur	Glum
góða	good
góðan	good
góðum	good
góma	gums
gott	god, good
gramir	anger
grán	grey
grandi	injury
greipur	grasp
greitt	ready-to-serve
gripur	treasure
gropasamlega	grouped-together
grösum	grass
gull	gold
gyllt	gold
gyltur	young-sow

H, h

Old Icelandic	English
háðs	mockery
háðungar	insult
hæð	height
hægra	easy
hætta	conclude, endanger
hætti	way
haf	sea
hafa	had, have
hafði	had
hafi	have
hafir	have
hagur	benefit, handy, skilled
halda	held, rather
haldi	hold
haldist	rather
hálft	half
hálfu	half
handkrækjumst	hands-hook-us
hann	he, him, it, 0
hans	he, him, his
Harald	Harald
Haraldi	Harald
Haralds	Harald's
Haraldur	Harald, Harald's
harðleikið	hardness
hart	hard
háttung	risk

Word List (Old Icelandic to English)

Old Icelandic	English	Old Icelandic	English
hefði	having	*hittir*	found
hefi	have	*hjá*	beside, by
hefir	had, has, have	*hlægi*	ridicule
hefnt	revenge	*hlæjandi*	laughing
heftir	have	*hlær*	laughed
heilinn	brain	*hleypur*	ran
heill	a-complete, the-whole, whole	*hljóp*	ran
heim	home	*hljóta*	luck
heima	at-home	*hló*	laughed
heimil	home	*hlotið*	bound-to
heitir	is-named	*hlut*	matter, share
heldur	behold, rather	*hluta*	share
heljar	death	*hlutar*	share
helst	rather	*hlutur*	share
hendi	hand	*hlýða*	listened
hendur	hand	*hlýdduð*	listen-to
hentu	handed	*hóf*	in-moderation
hentur	suited	*höfði*	head
hér	here	*höfðinu*	head
herbergi	room	*höfðu*	had
herra	lord	*hófi*	measure
hest	horse	*höfum*	have
hesta	horse	*hógvær*	humble
hestinn	the-horse	*hökulbrókum*	ankle-breeches
hestum	horses	*hólminn*	the-island
hestur	a-horse	*hólmur*	small-island
hesturinn	horse's	*hönd*	hand
hét	promised, was-named	*höndin*	hand
heyra	heard	*höndum*	handed, seized
heyrði	heard	*honum*	he, him, it
heyrir	heard	*horn*	corners
heyrt	heard	*hornblástur*	trumpet-blast
hið	that, the, to	*hræddur*	worried
hinn	the	*Hreiðar*	Hreidar
hinnug	there	*Hreiðari*	Hreidar
hirðarinnar	court	*Hreiðars*	Hreidar
hirðinni	court, court-men	*Hreiðarssonar*	Son-of-Hreidar
hirðmaður	court-man	*Hreiðarsstöðum*	Hreidar's-Place
hirðmann	court-man	*hríð*	awhile
hirðmönnum	court-men	*hring*	a-ring
hirðvistar	court, court-visit	*hrundu*	teased
hitt	find, it, this	*hrutu*	fell
hitta	meet	*hug*	thought
hittast	met	*hugði*	thought
hitti	met	*hugkvæmir*	very-smart

Word List (Old Icelandic to English)

Old Icelandic	English
hugkvæmur	ingenuity
hugur	think
hún	it
hurðina	the-door
húsi	house
hvað	how, what
hvar	where
hve	how
hver	each, every, what
hvergi	nowhere
hverju	what
hverjum	each, everyone
hvern	each, who
hvernug	how, which
hversu	how-so
hví	why
hvíldar	rest
hvort	how, whether
hygg	minded
hyggðu	think
hyggur	considered, looked, think

I, i

illa	badly
illt	bad, badly, ill
inn	in
innast	do

Í, í

í	as, at, by, from, in, of, so, the, to, with
Ísland	Iceland
Íslands	Iceland
íslendingar	icelander

J, j

já	yes
jafnan	always, equally
jafnmæli	equal-speak
jafnt	equally
jafnvel	equally-well

K, k

Old Icelandic	English
kæja	disturbed
kæmi	came
kæmir	come
kæmist	come
kallaður	called
kallar	called
kann	can, know
kaupa	buy
kemur	came
kenna	knew
kjósa	choose
klæðum	clothes
kné	knees
kom	came, come
koma	came, come, coming, to-come
komi	come
komið	came, come
kominn	came, come, coming
komnir	coming
komu	came
konung	the-king
konunga	kings
konungar	kings, the-kings
konungi	the-king
konunginn	the-king
konungs	king, the-king, the-king's
konungur	king, the-king
krummur	hands
kvað	said, spoke
kvæði	poem, the-poem
kvæðið	poem, the-poem
kvæðislaunin	poem-reward
kveðju	greeting
kveður	greeted, recited, spoke
kykvendum	some-beast
kynjalæti	eccentricities
kynleg	strange

Word List (Old Icelandic to English)

Old Icelandic	English
kynlegast	strangely
kynlegu	strange

L, l

Old Icelandic	English
læti	noise
lætur	had, leaves
lagði	had
lagður	had, laid
lagi	lead
land	land
landi	the-land
langar	long
langt	long
lát	have
láta	allow, be, be-allowed, have, left
latlega	negligently
lattan	dissuade
látum	have
launungu	secretly
laust	let-go
leggi	take
leggja	allow, let
leggur	have, laid
leið	way
leiðast	carried-out, hand
leik	sport
leikmikill	playful
leikurinn	the-game
leit	looked
leitað	sought
lék	played
lends	land
lengi	long
lést	let
lét	had
létu	had
leyfa	allow
leyfi	leave
leyfir	leave
leyft	given-leave
leysi	redeem
liði	company
liðs	company
liðu	passed
líður	passed, passes
líkar	like, liked
líkast	like
líklegt	favourable
líkur	like
líst	appears
líta	company
lítið	little
lítill	a-little, small
lítils	little
litlu	a-little
litu	noticed
ljótari	uglier
ljótur	ugly
ljúga	lie
lofgjarnlega	praise-will
loft	lift
lögðu	had
lokið	ended
lokka	lure
lundhægur	even-spirit, tempered-even
lýkur	concluded

M, m

Old Icelandic	English
má	may
maður	a-man, man, people
maðurinn	a-man
mæl	say
mæla	discuss
mælgina	talking
mæli	speak
mælir	spoke
mælt	speaking, spoken
mælti	said, spoke
mæltir	speak
mæltu	spoke
mætti	may
Magnús	Magnus
Magnúsi	Magnus
Magnúss	Magnus, Magnus's
mál	matter, matters, way
máli	speak

Word List (Old Icelandic to English)

Old Icelandic	English
málið	discuss
málinu	the-matter
málugur	talkative
mann	man, that-man
manna	a-man, men, people, the-men
mannfátt	people-few
manni	of-the-people
manninn	the-man
manninum	the-people
mannraunum	human-trials
manns	man
marga	many
margir	many
margs	many
mark	sign
mart	many
mast	most
mátti	it-may
máttu	may, may-you
með	among, as, with
mega	may
meiddur	hurt
meir	further, more
meira	more
menn	men, people
mennskur	human
mér	i, me, mine, my, to-me
mest	most
mesta	most
mestum	most
miðlung	poorly
mig	i, me, much
mikið	large, many, much
mikil	much
mikill	a-great, great, tall
mikinn	great
miklum	much
milli	between
mín	me, mine
mína	mine
mínar	mine
minn	mine
minna	less
minni	less
míns	mine
mitt	me, mine, my
mjög	much
mönnum	men, people
mörgu	many-ways
mörgum	many
morgun	morning
morguninn	morning
mót	against
móti	meeting, of
mótið	meeting, meetings
mótinu	meeting
móts	meet, meetings
mun	could, may, must, shall, should, would
muna	should
mund	time
mundi	should, would
mundir	would
muni	should, would
munni	mouth
munt	shall-you, should-you
muntu	shall-you
munu	shall

N, n

Old Icelandic	English
naddar	studded
nær	near
nakkvað	some
nakkvara	some
nakkvarri	some
nálægir	near-lying
námu	took
nauðsyn	need
nema	except
nemur	took
nestlokum	the-end
niður	down
njót	enjoy
nokkuð	of-any, some, something
nokkur	somewhat
norður	north
Noreg	Norway

Word List (Old Icelandic to English)

Old Icelandic	English	*Old Icelandic*	English
Noregi	Norway		
nú	now		
nýkominn	newly-come		
nýt	used		
nytjar	use		

O, o

Ö, ö

Old Icelandic	English
ofar	above
ofsögum	off-said
oft	frequently
og	also, and
okkað	ours
okkarn	ours
okkur	ours, us, you
orð	words
orðið	words
orðsending	message
orðum	words
orðvar	discreet
ort	worded
oss	us

öðru	others
öðrum	other, others
öllu	all
öllum	all
öngar	no
öngri	no
öngu	none
öxarsköft	axe-handles

P, p

peninga	money

Ó, ó

R, r

óbúinn	unprepared
ófælinn	without-fear
ógreið	un-passable
óheilagur	unholy
óknáleik	prowess
ólatur	not-forget
ólið	unaccompanied
ólíkast	unlike
ólíklegt	unlikely
ómállatur	chatty, talkative
ónýtt	ruined
ósannlegt	untrue
ósýknlegur	un-innocent-looking
óvanur	un-accustomed
óvart	un-warned
óvísu	unknown

ráð	advice, advised, decide
ráða	advice, advise, decide, decision
ráðlegra	advisable
ræða	discuss
ræðu	speech
rammur	frame
réði	decide
reið	rode
reiðar	ride
reiðast	anger
reiðfara	voyage
reiði	anger
reiðin	uproar
reiðina	anger
reiðingum	uproar
reiðist	angered, become-angry
reiður	angry
reikuð	roughly-handled
rennur	run
reyna	test
reynt	tried
rjáður	worried

Word List (Old Icelandic to English)

Old Icelandic	English

S, s

Old Icelandic	English
sá	saw, so, such, that
sæi	see
sæki	conviction
sæmilega	well-enough
sætt	settled, settlement
sættir	settle
sagði	said
sagt	said, told
sakar	conviction
sakir	reasons
sama	himself
saman	together
samdægris	same-day
samir	in-common
samtengja	unite
sanna	truth
sannast	true
satt	true
sáttarfundar	peace-meeting
sáttarfundur	peace-meeting
sáttir	agreed
sátu	sat
saurgar	dirty
sé	as, be, being, he, is, see, seeing, seen, so, you
séð	seen
sefur	sleeps
seg	tell
segir	said, say, told, 0
segja	said, say, told
seint	slowly
selji	sell
selur	sell
sem	as, how, like, such, which
senda	send, sending
sendan	sent
sendi	send, sent
senn	they, together
sér	he, him, himself, his, saw, so
sérð	saw, see
setur	set
séu	as
sex	six
síðan	after, afterwards, then
síðar	afterwards
síður	less
sig	him, himself, such, themselves
sigla	sailed
silfri	silver
silfrið	silver
silfur	silver
sín	theirs
sína	he, his
sinn	his, occasion
sinni	his, this
sínum	his
sitja	sit, sitting
sitt	his
sjá	saw, see, seemed, seen, so, to-see
sjálfan	myself
sjálfbjargi	self-supported
sjálfir	themselves
sjálfur	himself, self, yourself
skal	shall, should
skálpana	scabbards
skaltu	shall-you
skammt	short-distance
skap	mood
skapi	character
skauttogaður	roughly
skauttoguðu	pull-cloak, handle-roughly
skeindist	scratched
skerum	cut
skikkju	cloak
skikkjuna	cloak
skildi	parted
skildir	parted
skildust	separated
skilja	parted, understand
skilst	separate
skip	ship
skipa	exchange
skipast	changed

Word List (Old Icelandic to English)

Old Icelandic	English
skipdráttar	ship-launching
skjótt	swiftly
skógar	woods
skógum	the-woods
skömmu	recently
skortir	shortage
skrúðklæðin	costly-clothing
skulir	should
skulu	shall
skulum	shall, should
skýla	protect
skyldast	obliged
skyldi	should
skyldu	should
skýtur	throws
slíkt	such
sló	struck
smátt	small
smíðað	crafted, made, smithery
smíðaði	making
smíðinni	smith, the-work
snemma	early
sögðu	said
sögu	story
sökum	blame, sake
sönnu	true
sótti	took
spenar	suckling
spotti	small
spurði	asked
spyr	asked, learned
stað	place
staðinn	standing
stæði	stand
standa	stand, standing
standi	stand
stefnt	located
stendur	stood
sterkur	strong
stofuna	the-room
stofunni	the-room
stórvirkja	great-work
stukku	leapt
stund	awhile, time
stundir	while
stundu	time
stundum	awhile, sometimes
svaraði	answered
svarar	answered
Svarfaðardal	Svarfardal
sverðskónum	sword-studded
svín	a-pig
svínið	the-pig
svíninu	the-pig
svo	seen, so
sýnir	showed
sýnist	seemed, seems

T, t

Old Icelandic	English
tak	take
taka	take
tákna	betoken
táknar	taken
tal	talk
tala	talk
talað	told
tek	took
tekur	take, took
tíðinda	news
tíðindi	news
tíðir	wish
tigu	tens
til	to, until
tilgerðir	to-do
tjáir	express
tók	took
töluðu	talked
torsótt	difficulty
trautt	scarcely
treystist	we-trust
tröll	monstrous
trúi	trust
tvo	two
tvö	two

Word List (Old Icelandic to English)

Old Icelandic	English

Þ, þ

Old Icelandic	English
þá	then
það	is, it, that, the, this
þaðan	from-there
þætti	seemed, seems
þættist	we-have
þangað	from-here, there
þann	he, then
þannug	thus
þar	then, there, they
þarftu	need-you
þars	there
þau	then
þaut	shrill
þegar	already, as-soon, as-soon-as, from-there, soon, straightaway, then, there, when
þegi	silent
þeim	the, them, they
þeir	their, they
þeirra	them, they
þenna	that
þér	to-you, you, your
þess	this
þessa	this
þessarar	this-kind-of
þessi	these, this
þessir	these
þessu	this
þessum	this
þetta	that, this
þeygi	yet-not
þig	you
þín	you, yours
þína	your, yours
þingið	assembly
þingsins	their-assembly
þinn	your, yours
þitt	the, your, yours
þó	though
Þórð	Thord
Þórðar	Thord's
Þórði	Thord
Þórður	Thord
Þorgrímsson	Son-of-Thorgrim
þótt	though, thought
þótti	thought
þóttist	thought
þraut	faltered
þreytti	tired
þrotinn	ended
þú	though, you
þurfa	need, needed
þvarr	decreased
þvegnar	to-wash
því	accordingly, because, before, for, otherwise, since, such, then, therefore, this
þvílíkt	therefore-like
þykir	felt, seemed, think, thought
þykist	seems, think, thought
þykja	to-think
þykjast	consider

U, u

Old Icelandic	English
um	about, around
umbóta	put-right
umsjá	about, guidance
undan	away, away-from
undarlega	strange
undarlegt	wonderful
undarlegur	a-strange
undir	under
unga	young
unnið	done
uns	until
upp	up
upplönd	uplands
uppstert	upright
utan	out

Word List (Old Icelandic to English)

Old Icelandic	English

Ú, ú

úr	out-of
út	away, out
úti	out

V, v

vaðmál	homespun-cloth
vaðmálsklæði	wadding-clothes
vænleikur	handsome
vænn	handsome
vænsta	good
væri	was, were, will-be
væria	be
værir	be
væru	were
vaki	wake
vaknaðir	woken
valdið	wielded
vanbúinn	unprepared
vandamál	disputes
vandara	important
vandlega	closely
vandlegar	carefully
vant	difficult
var	aware, was, were
varla	hardly, scarcely
vasklegur	valiant
vega	ways
veggur	a-wall
vegið	slain
vegur	proceeded
veislu	feast
veistu	know-you
veit	knew, know, knows
veitt	given
veittir	grant
vel	well
vélir	wilful
velja	will
ver	be
vér	we
vera	be, become, being
verð	worth
verða	be, became, become, was
verði	became, become, becomes, was
verður	became, become, becomes, were
verið	been
verr	worse
verri	worse
verst	worse
vetri	winter
veturvistar	winter-provisions
vexti	grown
við	against, as, from, of, to, we, with
víðförull	widely-travelled
víginu	the-slaying
vil	will, wish
vildi	willed, wish, wished
vildir	would
vildu	wiled
vilgis	very
vilja	wish-to
vill	well, will, wished, wishes, would
vilt	will, wish
viltu	will-you, wish-you
vináttu	friendship
vindli	wind
vinveitt	friendly
virðir	worth
viskumaður	wise-man
vist	hospitality
víst	certainly
vistin	stay
vísu	certainly
vit	know
vita	know, knowing
viti	knowing
vitrari	wiser
vits	wits
viturlegra	wisely
vó	killed
vonir	custom
vopnum	weapons

Word List (Old Icelandic to English)

Old Icelandic	English
vor	ours
vorn	ours
voru	were

Y, y

yðarn	you
yður	you, your
yðvars	yours
yfir	about, over
ykkar	you
ykkur	you

Ý, ý

ýmsu	variously

Word List *(English to Old Icelandic)*

English	*Old Icelandic*	English	*Old Icelandic*
A, a		at-home	*heima*
		a-horse	*hestur*
about	*á, á, á, á*	ankle-breeches	*hökulbrókum*
at	*á, á, á*	awhile	*hríð, hring, hrutu*
a	*að, að*	a-ring	*hring*
as	*að, að, að, að, að, áðan, áður, áður*	always	*jafnan*
		allow	*láta, láta, láta*
after	*áður, áður, ætla*	appears	*líst*
aggression	*ágang*	a-little	*lítill, lítils*
age	*aldri*	a-man	*maður, maður, maðurinn*
all	*alla, allan, allgóð, allir, allnær, allra, allra, allríflegt, alls, allstarsýnn*	among	*með*
		a-great	*mikill*
		against	*mót, móti*
all-good	*allgóð*	above	*ofar*
all-near	*allnær*	also	*og*
all-abundant	*allríflegt*	axe-handles	*öxarsköft*
altogether	*allt*	advice	*ráð, ráð*
all-wonderful	*allundarlegt*	advised	*ráð*
all-well	*allvel, allvel,*	advise	*ráða*
all-the-people	*alþýðu*	advisable	*ráðlegra*
another	*annar*	angered	*reiðist*
any-other-place	*annarstaðar*	angry	*reiður*
asked	*beiddist, beiðir, beiðst, beiðst, ber*	agreed	*sáttir*
		answered	*svaraði, svarar*
ask	*biðja*	a-pig	*svín*
a-brother	*bróður*	already	*þegar*
away	*brott, brottu, brýst, búa*	as-soon	*þegar*
		as-soon-as	*þegar*
and	*eða, eða, eða, ef*	assembly	*þingið*
afterwards	*eftir, eg, eg*	accordingly	*því*
alone	*einn, einrænlegu*	around	*um*
am	*em, en*	a-strange	*undarlegur*
am-i	*er*	aware	*var*
are	*er, er, er, er, er*	a-wall	*veggur*
are-you	*ertu*		
away-from	*frá, frá*	**B, b**	
ahead	*fyrir*		
along	*fyrir*	by	*á, á, á*
amuse	*gamni*	been	*að, að*
anger	*gramir, grán, grandi, greipur*	before	*áður, ætla, ætlaði, ætlar, ævi*
a-complete	*heill*		

Word List (English to Old Icelandic)

English	*Old Icelandic*	English	*Old Icelandic*
back	aftur		
both	báðir, bæði		
bearing	bærist		
banned	banni		
beat	barður		
better	batna, beiddist, beiðir		
best	beiðst, ber		
bear	ber, ber, ber		
bite-bone	bitbeini		
Bergen	Björgyn		
brothers	bræðrum, bræður		
brother	bræður, bræður, brjóta		
break	brjóta		
bad	dála, dauður		
but	eða, eða, ef, efnin		
be	er, er, er, er, er, er, er, era		
being	er, er, er		
business	erindi		
born	fæðist		
bring	færa, færð		
brought	færði, færður, færi		
be-gifted	gæfu		
became	gerist, gerst, gerst, gert		
benefit	hagur		
brain	heilinn		
behold	heldur		
beside	hjá		
bound-to	hlotið		
badly	illa, illt		
buy	kaupa		
be-allowed	láta		
between	milli		
become-angry	reiðist		
blame	sökum		
betoken	tákna		
because	því		
become	vera, vera, verða, verða		
becomes	verði, verður		

C, c

English	*Old Icelandic*
carry	ber
carrying	ber
compensation	bóta
clothing	búning
closed	byrgður
capable	fær
can	færð, færði
cleaned	fágar
cloak	feld, feldinum, felld, fellt
criticised	firna
crowded	fjölmennt
companionship	föruneyti
company	föruneytis, forvitni, fót, frá
curious	forvitni
could	getu, getur
completely	gjörla
conclude	hætta
court	hirðarinnar, hirðinni, hirðinni
court-men	hirðinni, hirðmaður
court-man	hirðmaður, hirðmann
court-visit	hirðvistar
corners	horn
considered	hyggur
came	kæmi, kæmir, kæmist, kallaður, kallar, kann, kann
come	kæmir, kæmist, kallaður, kallar, kann, kann, kaupa
called	kallaður, kallar
choose	kjósa
clothes	klæðum
coming	koma, komi, komið
carried-out	leiðast
concluded	lýkur
chatty	ómállatur
conviction	sæki, sakar
character	skapi
cut	skerum
changed	skipast
costly-clothing	skrúðklæðin

105

Word List (English to Old Icelandic)

English	Old Icelandic
crafted	*smíðað*
consider	*þykjast*
closely	*vandlega*
carefully	*vandlegar*
certainly	*víst, vísu*
custom	*vonir*

D, d

English	Old Icelandic
dealings	*afskipti*
dwelling	*bænum*
death	*banans, banni*
dress	*búa*
dressed	*búinn*
dead	*dauður*
draw	*draga*
drawn	*dregst*
drinking	*drykkju*
disguise	*dylja*
drifted	*fauk*
did	*gera, gera, gera*
do	*gera, gera, geri*
done	*gera, geri, gerir, gerir*
disturbed	*kæja*
dissuade	*lattan*
discuss	*mæla, mætti, Magnús*
down	*niður*
discreet	*orðvar*
decide	*ráð, ráða, ráða*
decision	*ráða*
dirty	*saurgar*
decreased	*þvarr*
difficulty	*torsótt*
disputes	*vandamál*
difficult	*vant*

E, e

English	Old Icelandic
earlier	*áðan*
eye	*auga*
either	*eða*
especially	*einkum*
eccentric	*einrænlegu*
errand	*erindið*
Eyjafjord	*Eyjafirði*
Eyvind	*Eyvindar, Eyvindur*
end	*felld*
exceedingly-skilful	*geysihaglega*
easy	*hægra*
endanger	*hætta*
each	*hver, hver, hverjum*
every	*hver*
everyone	*hverjum*
equally	*jafnan, jafnmæli*
equal-speak	*jafnmæli*
equally-well	*jafnvel*
eccentricities	*kynjalæti*
ended	*lokið, lokka*
even-spirit	*lundhægur*
except	*nema*
enjoy	*njót*
exchange	*skipa*
early	*snemma*
express	*tjáir*

F, f

English	Old Icelandic
for	*á, á, á*
from	*á, á, á, að, að, að, að*
fool	*afglapa*
fixed-upon	*allstarsýnn*
few	*fáir, fallið*
fallen	*fallið, fallin*
found	*fann, fara, fara, farar, farið, farið*
fared	*farið*
fee	*fé*
falling	*fellt*
fell	*fellur, fenginn*
find	*finn, finna, finna, finnast, finnast*
fiendish	*fjandlegur*
followers	*fjölmenni*
followers-many	*fjölmenni*
for-travelling	*förin*
foot	*fót*
from-game	*fráleik*
follow	*fylgið, fylgjusamur*
follow-same	*fylgjusamur*

Word List (English to Old Icelandic)

English	*Old Icelandic*	English	*Old Icelandic*
fore-done	*fyrirgert*	great	*mikill, mikinn*
first	*fyrst, fyrstu*	great-work	*stórvirkja*
fun	*gaman*	guidance	*umsjá*
favourable	*líklegt*	grant	*veittir*
further	*meir*	grown	*vexti*
frequently	*oft*		
frame	*rammur*		
from-there	*þaðan, þangað*		
from-here	*þangað*		
faltered	*þraut*		
felt	*þykir*		
feast	*veislu*		
friendship	*vináttu*		
friendly	*vinveitt*		

H, h

English	*Old Icelandic*
has	*á, á, að*
had	*átt, átt, átti, auga, báðir, bæði, bænum, bærist, banans, banni, barður, batna, beiddist*
have	*átt, átti, auga, báðir, bæði, bænum, bærist, banans, banni, barður, batna, beiddist, beiðir*
hammering	*brýst*
height	*hæð*
handy	*hagur*
held	*halda*
hold	*haldi*
half	*hálft, hálfu*
hands-hook-us	*handkrækjumst*
he	*hann, hann, hann, hans, hans, hans, Harald*
him	*hann, hann, hans, hans, hans*
his	*hans, Harald, Haraldi, Haralds, Haraldur, Haraldur, harðleikið*
Harald	*Harald, Haraldi, Haralds*
Harald's	*Haralds, Haraldur*
hardness	*harðleikið*
hard	*hart*
having	*hefði*
home	*heim, heima*
hand	*hendi, hendur, hentu, hér, herra*
handed	*hentu, hér*
here	*hér*
horse	*hest, hesta*
horses	*hestum*

G, g

English	*Old Icelandic*
get	*fá, fá*
give	*fá, fæ, fæðist, fær*
go	*fara, fara, farar, farið, farið, farið, fátt*
going	*fara, farar, farið, farið, farið, fátt*
given	*fenginn, fer*
goes	*fer*
group	*flokk*
game	*fráleikurinn, fram*
good-things	*fríðinda*
got	*gæti, gaf, gafst*
gave	*gaf, gafst, gaman, gaman*
guess	*get*
Glum	*Glúmur*
good	*góða, góðan, góðum, góma, gott*
gums	*góma*
god	*gott*
grey	*grán*
grasp	*greipur*
grouped-together	*gropasamlega*
grass	*grösum*
gold	*gull, gyllt*
greeting	*kveðju*
greeted	*kveður*
given-leave	*leyft*

Word List (English to Old Icelandic)

English	*Old Icelandic*	English	*Old Icelandic*
horse's	*hesturinn*	in-common	*samir*
heard	*heyra, heyrði, heyrir, heyrt*	important	*vandara*
head	*höfði, höfðinu*		
humble	*hógvær*		
Hreidar	*Hreiðar, Hreiðari, Hreiðars*	## J, j	
Hreidar's-Place	*Hreiðarsstöðum*	joyfully	*blíðlega*
house	*húsi*	journey	*farar*
how	*hvað, hve, hver, hver, hverjum*	## K, k	
how-so	*hversu*		
hands	*krummur*	kill	*drepa, drepi, drepið*
human-trials	*mannraunum*	killed	*drepinn, drykkju*
hurt	*meiddur*	kinsman	*frændi*
human	*mennskur*	kinsmen	*frændi*
himself	*sama, samir, sáttir, saurgar*	know	*kann, kaupa, kemur, kenna*
homespun-cloth	*vaðmál*	knew	*kenna, kjósa*
handsome	*vænleikur, vænn*	knees	*kné*
hardly	*varla*	kings	*konunga, konungar*
hospitality	*vist*	king	*konungs, konungur*
		know-you	*veistu*
## I, i		knows	*veit*
		knowing	*vita, viti*
in	*á, að, að, að, að*		
is	*að, áðan, áður, áður, ætla*	## L, l	
intended	*ætla, ætlaði, ætlar*		
if	*ef*	life	*ævi*
i	*eg, eg, eiga, eiga, einkum*	lived	*bjó*
		little	*fátt, fauk, fé*
is-not	*ekki*	last-years	*fyrra*
inheritance	*föðurarf*	lord	*herra*
in-front-of	*fyrir*	laughing	*hlæjandi*
injury	*grandi*	laughed	*hlær, hljóta*
insult	*háðungar*	luck	*hljóta*
it	*hann, hans, hans, hans, Harald*	listened	*hlýða*
		listen-to	*hlýdduð*
is-named	*heitir*	looked	*hyggur, í*
in-moderation	*hóf*	leaves	*lætur*
ingenuity	*hugkvæmur*	laid	*lagður, lagi*
ill	*illt*	lead	*lagi*
Iceland	*Ísland, Íslands*	land	*land, langar*
icelander	*íslendingar*	long	*langar, langt, lát*
it-may	*mátti*	left	*láta*

Word List (English to Old Icelandic)

English	Old Icelandic
let-go	*laust*
let	*leggja, leggur*
leave	*leyfi, leyfir*
like	*líkar, líkar, líkast, líklegt*
liked	*líkar*
lie	*ljúga*
lift	*loft*
lure	*lokka*
large	*mikið*
less	*minna, minni, míns*
learned	*spyr*
located	*stefnt*
leapt	*stukku*

M, m

English	Old Icelandic
materials	*efnin*
money	*fé, feld*
monstrous	*ferlegu, finn*
meet	*finnast, finnast, finnast, finnst*
meet-up	*finnast*
met	*finnast, finnst, finnumst*
many-people	*fjölmennið*
most	*flesta, flokk, fluttir, föðurarf, för*
made	*ger, gera, gera, gera, geri*
mention	*get*
mocking	*ginna, ginningar*
mockery	*háðs*
matter	*hlut, hlýða*
measure	*hófi*
minded	*hygg*
may	*má, maður, maður, maðurinn, mæla*
man	*maður, maðurinn, mæla*
Magnus	*Magnús, Magnúsi, Magnúss*
Magnus's	*Magnúss*
matters	*mál*
men	*manna, mannraunum, manns*
many	*marga, margir, margs, mart, mast, mátti*
may-you	*máttu*
more	*meir, meira*
me	*mér, mér, mér, mest*
mine	*mér, mér, mest, mesta, mestum, mig, mig*
my	*mér, mest*
much	*mig, mikið, mikið, mikið, mikil*
many-ways	*mörgu*
morning	*morgun, morguninn*
meeting	*móti, mótið, mótið*
meetings	*mótið, mótinu*
must	*mun*
mouth	*munni*
message	*orðsending*
myself	*sjálfan*
mood	*skap*
making	*smíðaði*

N, n

English	Old Icelandic
never	*aldregi, aldrei, aldrei*
numb	*dofna*
none	*eigi, eigi, eigi*
not	*eigi, eigi, eigi*
nothing	*eigi*
no	*engi, engi, engi*
no-one	*engi*
news	*fréttir, fund, fundar*
nowhere	*hvergi*
noise	*læti*
negligently	*latlega*
noticed	*litu*
near	*nær*
near-lying	*nálægir*
need	*nauðsyn, nemur*
north	*norður*
Norway	*Noreg, Noregi*
now	*nú*
newly-come	*nýkominn*
not-forget	*ólatur*
need-you	*þarftu*

Word List (English to Old Icelandic)

English	*Old Icelandic*
needed	þurfa

O, o

English	*Old Icelandic*
of	á, á, á, á, á, á, að, að
on	á, á
other	aðra, aðrir, áður, ætla, ætlar
others	aðrir, áður, ætla
of-life	ævinnar
off	af
offer	búnir
or	eða
own	eiga, eigi
one-thing	eigi
once	einhverju, einn
one	einn, eins, einum, eirir
one's	eins
otherwise	ellegar, elli
old-age	elli
of-wealth	fjárins
of-the-people	manni
of-any	nokkuð
off-said	ofsögum
ours	okkað, okkarn, okkur, okkur, okkur
occasion	sinn
obliged	skyldast
out-of	úr
out	út, utan, úti
over	yfir

P, p

English	*Old Icelandic*
place-about	ásáttir
prepared	bjó, bjó, blásið
prepare	bú
passed	fer, fer, fer
promised	hét
poem	kvæði, kvæði
poem-reward	kvæðislaunin
playful	leikmikill
played	lék
passes	líður

English	*Old Icelandic*
praise-will	lofgjarnlega
people	maður, mæl, mælgina, mæli
people-few	mannfátt
poorly	miðlung
prowess	óknáleik
peace-meeting	sáttarfundar, sáttarfundur
pull-cloak, handle-roughly	skauttoguðu
parted	skildi, skildir, skildust
protect	skýla
place	stað
put-right	umbóta
proceeded	vegur

R, r

English	*Old Icelandic*
returned	áður
rough	álpun
residence	bænum
ready-to-serve	greitt
rather	halda, haldist, háttung, hefnt
risk	háttung
revenge	hefnt
room	herbergi
ridicule	hlægi
ran	hleypur, hljóp
rest	hvíldar
recited	kveður
redeem	leysi
ruined	ónýtt
rode	reið
ride	reiðar
roughly-handled	reikuð
run	rennur
reasons	sakir
roughly	skauttogaður
recently	skömmu

S, s

English	*Old Icelandic*
so	á, á, á, á, að, að, að
suppose	ætla, ætlar, ætlun

Word List (English to Old Icelandic)

English	*Old Icelandic*	English	*Old Icelandic*
stood-out	*afbragð*	some	*nakkvað, nakkvara, nakkvarri, nálægir*
strength	*afl, afli, aflið*		
settled	*bjó, blásið, borðið*	something	*nokkuð*
soon	*brátt, breyttu*	somewhat	*nokkur*
steep	*brottu*	speech	*ræðu*
secure	*fastur*	saw	*sá, sá, sá, sá*
shed	*felld*	such	*sá, sá, sæi, sæmilega, sætt*
situated	*felldur*		
sacrificing	*förina*	see	*sæi, sæmilega, sætt, sætt*
self-control	*forræði*		
swiftness	*fráleikurinn*	settlement	*sætt*
swift	*frávastur*	settle	*sættir*
sea	*haf*	same-day	*samdægris*
skilled	*hagur*	sat	*sátu*
suited	*hentur*	seeing	*sé*
share	*hlut, hluta, hlutar, hlutur*	seen	*sé, sé, sé, séð*
		sleeps	*sefur*
small-island	*hólmur*	slowly	*seint*
seized	*höndum*	sell	*selji, selur*
Son-of-Hreidar	*Hreiðarssonar*	send	*senda, senda*
said	*kvað, kvað, kvæði, kvæði, kvæðið, kvæðið, kvæðislaunin*	sending	*senda*
		sent	*sendan, sendi*
		set	*setur*
spoke	*kvað, kvæði, kvæði, kvæðið, kvæðið*	six	*sex*
		sailed	*sigla*
some-beast	*kykvendum*	silver	*silfri, silfrið, silfur*
strange	*kynleg, kynlegast, kynlegu*	sit	*sitja*
		sitting	*sitja*
strangely	*kynlegast*	seemed	*sjá, sjá, sjá, sjá*
secretly	*launungu*	self-supported	*sjálfbjargi*
sport	*leik*	self	*sjálfur*
sought	*leitað*	scabbards	*skálpana*
small	*lítill, litu, ljótari*	short-distance	*skammt*
say	*mæl, mælgina, mæli*	scratched	*skeindist*
speak	*mæli, mælir, mælt*	separated	*skildust*
speaking	*mælt*	separate	*skilst*
spoken	*mælt*	ship	*skip*
sign	*mark*	ship-launching	*skipdráttar*
shall	*mun, mun, mun, muna, mund*	swiftly	*skjótt*
		shortage	*skortir*
should	*mun, mun, muna, mund, mundi, mundi, mundir, muni, muni*	struck	*sló*
		smithery	*smíðað*
		smith	*smíðinni*
		story	*sögu*
shall-you	*munt, munt, muntu*	sake	*sökum*
should-you	*munt*	suckling	*spenar*
studded	*naddar*		

111

Word List (English to Old Icelandic)

English	Old Icelandic	English	Old Icelandic
standing	staðinn, stæði	travelling	ferðina, fjárins, fjárskakka, fleygir
stand	stæði, standa, standa	threw	fleygir
stood	stendur	transport	flytur
strong	sterkur	trading-voyages	förum
sometimes	stundum	to-meet	fundar
Svarfardal	Svarfaðardal	the-meeting	fundarins
sword-studded	sverðskónum	taken-care-of	gætt
showed	sýnir	to-give	gefa
seems	sýnist, tak, taka	told	getið, greitt, gripur, gyltur, hætti
shrill	þaut	treasure	gripur
straightaway	þegar	the-whole	heill
silent	þegi	the-horse	hestinn
Son-of-Thorgrim	Þorgrímsson	there	hinnug, hitt, hlægi, hleypur, hljóp
since	því	this	hitt, hlægi, hleypur, hljóp, hlut, hluta, hlutar, hlutur, hólminn, hólmur
scarcely	trautt, treystist		
slain	vegið		
stay	vistin		

T, t

English	Old Icelandic	English	Old Icelandic
		the-island	hólminn
		teased	hrundu
that	á, á, á, að, að, að, að, að, að, að, aðra	thought	hug, hugði, hugkvæmir, hugur, hurðina, hvað, hvar
then	á, á, að, að, að, að, að, að, að, aðra, aðrir	think	hugur, hurðina, hvað, hvar, hver
to	á, að, að, að, að, að, að	the-door	hurðina
than	að, að	to-come	koma
the	að, að, að, aðra, aðrir, áður, ætla, ætlar, ætlun, ævinnar	the-king	konung, konungar, konungi, konunginn, konungs
to-hear	áheyrsli	the-kings	konungar
the-people	alþýðu, annað	the-king's	konungs
take-care-of	annast	the-poem	kvæði, kvæðið
to-ask	biðja	the-land	landi
trumpet-blast	blásið, borðið	take	leggi, leið, leik, leikmikill
table	borðið		
tricky	brögðóttur	the-game	leikurinn
to-deem	dæmd	tempered-even	lundhægur
to-kill	drepa	talking	mælgina
to-be	er, er	the-matter	málinu
they-are	eru	talkative	málugur, mann
to-go	fara	that-man	mann
travel	fara, fara, fara	the-men	manna
travelled	fara, fara, fara, fari, fari, fastur	the-man	manninn
		to-me	mér

Word List (English to Old Icelandic)

English	*Old Icelandic*
tall	*mikill*
time	*mund, mundi, mundi*
took	*námu, nauðsyn, nemur, nestlokum, nokkuð, nokkuð*
the-end	*nestlokum*
test	*reyna*
tried	*reynt*
together	*saman, samdægris*
truth	*sanna*
true	*sannast, satt, sáttarfundar*
tell	*seg*
they	*senn, senn, sér, sér, sérð*
themselves	*sig, sigla*
theirs	*sín*
to-see	*sjá*
the-woods	*skógum*
throws	*skýtur*
the-work	*smíðinni*
the-room	*stofuna, stofunni*
the-pig	*svínið, svíninu*
taken	*táknar*
talk	*tal, tala*
thus	*þannug*
them	*þeim, þeim*
their	*þeir*
to-you	*þér*
this-kind-of	*þessarar*
these	*þessi, þessi*
their-assembly	*þingsins*
though	*þó, Þórð, Þórðar*
Thord	*Þórð, Þórðar, Þórði*
Thord's	*Þórðar*
tired	*þreytti*
to-wash	*þvegnar*
therefore	*því*
therefore-like	*þvílíkt*
to-think	*þykja*
tens	*tigu*
to-do	*tilgerðir*
talked	*töluðu*
trust	*trúi*
two	*tvo, tvö*
the-slaying	*víginu*

U, u

English	*Old Icelandic*
uneven-share	*fjárskakka*
uglier	*ljótari*
ugly	*ljótur*
used	*nýt*
use	*nytjar*
unprepared	*óbúinn, öðru*
un-passable	*ógreið*
unholy	*óheilagur*
us	*okkur, okkur*
unaccompanied	*ólið*
unlike	*ólíkast*
unlikely	*ólíklegt*
untrue	*ósannlegt*
un-innocent-looking	*ósýknlegur*
un-accustomed	*óvanur*
un-warned	*óvart*
unknown	*óvísu*
uproar	*reiðin, reiðingum*
unite	*samtengja*
understand	*skilja*
until	*til, tilgerðir*
under	*undir*
up	*upp*
uplands	*upplönd*
upright	*uppstert*

V, v

English	*Old Icelandic*
very-timid	*alláræðislítill*
varied	*breyttu*
visit	*fund*
very-smart	*hugkvæmir*
voyage	*reiðfara*
valiant	*vasklegur*
very	*vilgis*
variously	*ýmsu*

Word List (English to Old Icelandic)

English	*Old Icelandic*	English	*Old Icelandic*
W, w		worth	*verð, verða*
		worse	*verr, verri, verst*
with	*að, aðra, aðrir, áður*	winter	*vetri*
when	*en, engi, engi*	winter-provisions	*veturvistar*
was	*er, er, er, er, er, er*	widely-travelled	*víðförull*
were	*er, er, er, er, er, er, er*	willed	*vildi*
what	*er, er, er, er*	wiled	*vildu*
where	*er, er*	wish-to	*vilja*
which	*er, er, er*	wishes	*vill*
who	*er, er*	will-you	*viltu*
whom	*er*	wish-you	*viltu*
would	*er, eru, eru, eru, fagna, fara, fara*	wind	*vindli*
		wise-man	*viskumaður*
welcomed	*fagna*	wiser	*vitrari*
went	*fara, fara, fari, fari, fastur, felld, felldur*	wits	*vits*
		wisely	*viturlegra*
wished	*fúsastur, gætt, ganga*	weapons	*vopnum*
walked	*gengur*		
way	*hætti, haf, hagur*	**Y, y**	
whole	*heill*		
was-named	*hét*	young-sow	*gyltur*
worried	*hræddur, Hreiðarssonar*	yes	*já*
		you	*okkur, óknáleik, ólatur, ólið, ólíkast, ólíklegt, ómállatur, öngar, öngri, öngu*
why	*hví*		
whether	*hvort*		
without-fear	*ófælinn*		
words	*orð, orðið, orðum*		
worded	*ort*	yourself	*sjálfur*
well-enough	*sæmilega*	your	*þér, þess, þessa, þessarar, þessi*
woods	*skógar*		
while	*stundir*	yet-not	*þeygi*
we-have	*þættist*	yours	*þín, þína, þína, þingsins, þinn*
wish	*tíðir, tigu, til, til*		
we-trust	*treystist*	young	*unga*
wonderful	*undarlegt*		
wadding-clothes	*vaðmálsklæði*		
will-be	*væri*		
wake	*vaki*		
woken	*vaknaðir*		
wielded	*valdið*		
ways	*vega*		
well	*vel, vélir*		
wilful	*vélir*		
will	*velja, vér, verð, verða*		
we	*vér, verð*		

A Word Comparison of Old Norse and Old Icelandic Words

Old Norse	Old Icelandic	English	Old Norse	Old Icelandic	English
áðr	áður	after	bræðr	bræður	brothers
áðr	áður	before	brögðóttr	brögðóttur	tricky
áðr	áður	returned	brýzt	brýst	hammering
ætlan	ætlun	suppose	búit	búið	settled
af	að	of	byrgðr	byrgður	closed
aflit	aflið	strength	dæmð	dæmd	to-deem
aftr	aftur	back	dauðr	dauður	dead
aftr	aftur	before	eigu	eiga	have
aldri	aldrei	never	einrænligu	einrænlegu	eccentric
aldrigi	aldregi	never	ek	eg	i
allr	allur	all	ek	eg	is
allrífligt	allríflegt	all-abundant	ekki	ekki,	not
allundarligt	allundarlegt	all-wonderful	elligar	ellegar	otherwise
allvel	allvel,	all-well	engar	öngar	no
annarr	annar	another	engri	öngri	no
annat	annað	other	engu	öngu	none
at	að	a	enn	en	but
at	að	as	erendi	erindi	business
at	að	at	erendit	erindið	errand
at	að	been	Eyvindr	Eyvindur	Eyvind
at	að	in	fær	færð	can
at	að	is	færðr	færður	brought
at	að	of	færr	fær	capable
at	að	on	fallit	fallið	fallen
at	að	than	fara	fari	travel
at	að	that	farit	farið	fared
at	að	the	farit	farið	going
at	að	to	fastr	fastur	secure
at	að	with	felldr	felldur	situated
at	athlægi	the	fellr	fellur	fell
barðr	barður	beat	ferligu	ferlegu	monstrous
beiðzt	beiðst	asked	ferr	fer	goes
beiðzt	beiðst	best	ferr	fer	passed
berr	ber	carry	ferr	fer	travelled
berr	ber	carrying	ferr	fer	went
betr	betur	better	fjandligr	fjandlegur	fiendish
bezt	best	best	fjölmennit	fjölmennið	many-people
blásit	blásið	trumpet-blast	flytr	flytur	transport
blíðlíga	blíðlega	joyfully	förna	förina	sacrificing
borðit	borðið	table	fráleikrinn	fráleikurinn	game
borit	borið	bear	fráleikrinn	fráleikurinn	swiftness

A Word Comparison of Old Norse and Old Icelandic

Old Norse	Old Icelandic	English	Old Norse	Old Icelandic	English
frávastr	frávastur	swift	hlutr	hlutur	share
fríðenda	fríðinda	good-things	hlýddið	hlýdduð	listen-to
fundit	fundið	found	hógværr	hógvær	humble
fúsastr	fúsastur	wished	hólmr	hólmur	small-island
fylgjusamr	fylgjusamur	follow-same	hon	hún	it
gefr	gefur	give	hornblástr	hornblástur	trumpet-blast
gengr	gengur	go	hræddr	hræddur	worried
gengr	gengur	going	Hreiðarr	Hreiðar	Hreidar
gengr	gengur	walked	hugkvæmr	hugkvæmur	ingenuity
gengr	gengur	went	hugr	hugur	think
gerik	geri	do	hvárt	hvort	how
gerla	gjörla	completely	hvárt	hvort	whether
gerr	ger	made	hvat	hvað	how
gerzt	gerst	done	hvat	hvað	what
gerzt	gerst	made	hvé	hve	how
getit	getið	told	hvernig	hvernug	how
getr	getur	get	hvernig	hvernug	which
geysihagliga	geysihaglega	exceedingly-skilful	hverr	hver	each
glíkligt	líklegt	favourable	hverr	hver	every
glíkr	líkur	like	hverr	hver	what
Glúmr	Glúmur	Glum	hyggr	hyggur	considered
greipr	greipur	grasp	hyggr	hyggur	looked
gripr	gripur	treasure	hyggr	hyggur	think
gropasamliga	gropasamlega	grouped-together	inn	hinn	the
gyltr	gyltur	young-sow	ísinn	sinn	his
hagr	hagur	benefit	it	hið	that
hagr	hagur	handy	it	hið	the
hagr	hagur	skilled	it	hið	to
Haraldr	Haraldur	Harald	kallaðr	kallaður	called
Haraldr	Haraldur	Harald's	kemr	kemur	came
harðleikit	harðleikið	hardness	komit	komið	came
heldr	heldur	behold	komit	komið	come
heldr	heldur	rather	kómu	komu	came
helzt	helst	rather	konungr	konungur	king
hendr	hendur	hand	konungr	konungur	the-king
hendu	hentu	handed	korn	kom	came
hentr	hentur	suited	kvæðit	kvæðið	poem
hestr	hestur	a-horse	kvæðit	kvæðið	the-poem
hestrinn	hesturinn	horse's	kveðr	kveður	greeted
heyrðak	heyrði	heard	kveðr	kveður	recited
hinnig	hinnug	there	kveðr	kveður	spoke
hirðmaðr	hirðmaður	court-man	kynlig	kynleg	strange
hleypr	hleypur	ran	kynligast	kynlegast	strangely
hlotit	hlotið	bound-to	kynligu	kynlegu	strange
			lætr	lætur	had

A Word Comparison of Old Norse and Old Icelandic

Old Norse	Old Icelandic	English	Old Norse	Old Icelandic	English
lætr	lætur	leaves	*mótit*	mótið	meetings
lagðr	lagður	had	*muna*	muni	should
lagðr	lagður	laid	*muntu*	munt	should-you
latliga	latlega	negligently	*myndi*	mundi	should
leggja	leggi	take	*myndi*	mundi	would
leggr	leggur	have	*myndir*	mundir	would
leggr	leggur	laid	*nemr*	nemur	took
leikrinn	leikurinn	the-game	*niðr*	niður	down
leitat	leitað	sought	*nökkur*	nokkur	somewhat
leysa	leysi	redeem	*nökkura*	nakkvara	some
lézt	lést	let	*nökkurri*	nakkvarri	some
líðr	líður	passed	*nökkut*	nakkvað	some
líðr	líður	passes	*nökkut*	nokkuð	of-any
líkr	líkur	like	*nökkut*	nokkuð	some
lítit	lítið	little	*nökkut*	nokkuð	something
lízt	líst	appears	*norðr*	norður	north
ljótr	ljótur	ugly	*Nóreg*	Noreg	Norway
lofgjarnliga	lofgjarnlega	praise-will	*Nóregi*	Noregi	Norway
lokit	lokið	ended	*óheilagr*	óheilagur	unholy
lundhægr	lundhægur	even-spirit	*ok*	og	also
lundhægr	lundhægur	tempered-even	*ok*	og	and
lýkr	lýkur	concluded	*okkart*	okkað	ours
maðr	maður	a-man	*okkr*	okkur	ours
maðr	maður	man	*okkr*	okkur	us
maðr	maður	people	*okkr*	okkur	you
maðrinn	maðurinn	a-man	*ökulbrókum*	hökulbrókum	ankle-breeches
mælik	mæli	speak	*ólatr*	ólatur	not-forget
mælir	mælti	spoke	*ólíkligt*	ólíklegt	unlikely
málit	málið	discuss	*ómállatr*	ómállatur	chatty
málugr	málugur	talkative	*ómállatr*	ómállatur	talkative
margt	mart	many	*ór*	úr	out-of
mazt	mast	most	*orðit*	orðið	words
meiddr	meiddur	hurt	*orðvarr*	orðvar	discreet
mennskr	mennskur	human	*ósannligt*	ósannlegt	untrue
miðlungi	miðlung	poorly	*ósýknligr*	ósýknlegur	un-innocent-looking
mik	mig	i			
mik	mig	me	*óvanr*	óvanur	un-accustomed
mik	mig	much	*penninga*	peninga	money
mikit	mikið	large	*ráðligra*	ráðlegra	advisable
mikit	mikið	many	*rammi*	rammur	frame
mikit	mikið	much	*reiðr*	reiður	angry
mjök	mjög	much	*reiðumst*	reiðist	become-angry
morgin	morgun	morning	*rennr*	rennur	run
morgininn	morguninn	morning	*rjáðr*	rjáður	worried
mótit	mótið	meeting	*sæja*	sæi	see

A Word Comparison of Old Norse and Old Icelandic

Old Norse	Old Icelandic	English	Old Norse	Old Icelandic	English
sæmiliga	sæmilega	well-enough	þættist	þóttist	thought
sagða	sagði	said	þættumst	þættist	we-have
sakar	sakir	reasons	þangat	þangað	from-here
sáttarfundr	sáttarfundur	peace-meeting	þangat	þangað	there
sé	séu	as	þannig	þannug	thus
sefr	sefur	sleeps	þat	það	is
selja	selji	sell	þat	það	it
selr	selur	sell	þat	það	that
sér	sérð	saw	þat	það	the
sér	sérð	see	þat	það	this
sét	séð	seen	þ-at	það	it
setr	setur	set	þeira	þeirra	them
síðr	síður	less	þeira	þeirra	they
sik	sig	him	þik	þig	you
sik	sig	himself	þingit	þingið	assembly
sik	sig	such	Þórðr	Þórði	Thord
sik	sig	themselves	Þórðr	Þórður	Thord
silfr	silfur	silver	þykkir	þykir	felt
silfrit	silfrið	silver	þykkir	þykir	seemed
sinn	sinni	his	þykkir	þykir	think
sjálfr	sjálfur	himself	þykkir	þykir	thought
sjálfr	sjálfur	self	þykkist	þykist	seems
sjálfr	sjálfur	yourself	þykkist	þykist	think
skauttogaðr	skauttogaður	roughly	þykkist	þykist	thought
skilði	skildi	parted	þykkja	þykja	to-think
skilðir	skildir	parted	þykkjast	þykjast	consider
skilðust	skildust	separated	þykkjumst	þykist	think
skyldi	skyldu	should	tíðenda	tíðinda	news
skýtr	skýtur	throws	tíðendi	tíðindi	news
smíðat	smíðað	crafted	treystumst	treystist	we-trust
smíðat	smíðað	made	tvá	tvo	two
smíðat	smíðað	smithery	tvau	tvö	two
spyrr	spyr	asked	undarliga	undarlega	strange
spyrr	spyr	learned	undarligr	undarlegur	a-strange
srterkr	sterkur	strong	undarligt	undarlegt	wonderful
stæða	stæði	stand	unnit	unnið	done
stendr	stendur	stood	unz	uns	until
sterkr	sterkur	strong	útan	utan	out
svá	svo	seen	vá	vó	killed
svá	svo	so	vælir	vélir	wilful
svínit	svínið	the-pig	vænleikr	vænleikur	handsome
sýndi	sýnir	showed	væri	væru	were
talat	talað	told	valdit	valdið	wielded
tekr	tekur	take	vandliga	vandlega	closely
tekr	tekur	took	vandligar	vandlegar	carefully

A Word Comparison of Old Norse and Old Icelandic

Old Norse	Old Icelandic	English
vánir	vonir	custom
vápnum	vopnum	weapons
várn	vorn	ours
varr	var	aware
várr	vor	ours
váru	voru	were
vaskligr	vasklegur	valiant
veggr	veggur	a-wall
vegit	vegið	slain
vegr	vegur	proceeded
veizlu	veislu	feast
veiztu	veistu	know-you
verðr	verður	became
verðr	verður	become
verðr	verður	becomes
verðr	verður	were
verit	verið	been
vetrvistar	veturvistar	winter-provisions
vilda	vildi	willed
vilda	vildi	wish
vilda	vildi	wished
vill	vilt	will
vill	vilt	wish
villt	vilt	wish
villtu	viltu	will-you
villtu	viltu	wish-you
vit	við	we
vitrligra	viturlegra	wisely
vizkumaðr	viskumaður	wise-man
yðr	yður	you
yðr	yður	your
yðvarn	yðarn	you
ykkr	ykkur	you

www.ingramcontent.com/pod-product-compliance
Lightning Source LLC
Chambersburg PA
CBHW051418070526
44584CB00023B/3487